**ANCHOR BOOKS**

To Tell A Story

Edited by

Heather Killingray

First published in Great Britain in 1998 by
ANCHOR BOOKS
1-2 Wainman Road, Woodston,
Peterborough, PE2 7BU
Telephone (01733) 230761

HB ISBN 1 85930 667 5
SB ISBN 1 85930 662 4

FOREWORD

Anchor Books is a small press, established in 1992, with the aim of promoting readable poetry to as wide an audience as possible.

We hope to establish an outlet for writers of poetry who may have struggled to see their work in print.

The poems presented here have been selected from many entries. Editing proved to be a difficult task and as the Editor, the final selection was mine.

I trust this selection will delight and please the authors and all those who enjoy reading poetry.

Heather Killingray
Editor

CONTENTS

MY GRANDSON

I often sigh with envy of my friends' posh tidy homes
Their gardens laid out neatly with their well-placed coloured gnomes.
Their windows gleam immaculate in the sun's bright shiny rays
Flowers arranged articulate in expensive crystal vase
Chairs with cushions plumped and tidy beckon to sit at ease
Carpets soft and fluffy - no shoe-scuffed marks on these!

Not for me this tranquil scene of peace and quiet - and pristine clean.
Mine is doors and windows smeared with sticky little hands
Biscuit crumbs and marks of thumb - wellies full of gritty sand.
Teletubbies videos are strewn across the floor
Teddy bears and Lego bricks- crayon scribble on the doors.

Where my friends can lie in blissful peace to enjoy a fragrant soak
My bath is filled with plastic boats and bright green frogs that croak.

My bed - though tidy at the start is soon in disarray
Pillows flattened with tiny feet - brushes and combs adorn the duvet.

My lawn is like a battle ground with scooters, trikes and trucks.
My garden pond is waterless with broken concrete ducks.

My friends may look with pity at my life with all its stress
Of, 'Don't do that,' and 'Mind the cat,' and 'Look at all that mess!'
But when a chubby little hand inside of mine I clutch
And two appealing baby eyes gaze at me with trust
There's nothing in this world I'd swap for that tender little touch
And a tiny voice that whispers, 'Nan, I love you very much.'

Elsie Francis

FAIRY TALE DREAMS

When I was a little girl,
And my Daddy was my hero,
I dreamed of being a princess,
In a fairy tale from long ago.

I was sure I'd meet my prince one day,
And live in a fairy castle,
Where roses grew around the door -
But I've had a little hassle!

Perhaps the wicked fairy cursed me,
Swearing that I've already enough,
For every time I kiss a prince,
He turns into a frog and not a love!

Perhaps I'd be better off sleeping,
For at least a hundred years,
Thorns would grow over my lips,
Warning princes of her curse.

And now that I'm a grown up girl,
I dream of fairy godmothers at night,
Hoping one will wave her wand,
And I'll meet my Prince Right!

Either way, my Daddy's still my hero,
And I know I'll always be his princess,
So even if I meet my prince,
I won't love my Daddy any less!

Claire Angharad

HILL VISITORS

We have come all this way,
For nothing, would you say?
Tramped over hills along rough tracks
Among the purple heather.

To get, to hold, to have
How this can be so sad!
Is this the main desire,
To travel all these miles?

There is a finer thought,
And that which we have sought
To look, to see and meditate
On life's wonders to behold.

For in the transient moments of the day
See things joyous with delight we may.
See the glowing sunset behind the waves
Hear the gentle swish of an inshore breeze.

There is quietness that gives us pleasure.
Nature's clear fresh air is there to treasure.
Before we return to our homes,
We have seen with memories to remember.

Mary Cornelius

WHEN YOU WERE MINE

We were busy people with lots going on
late to bed and up at dawn
weeks went by, we hardly knew it
no time to read or contemplate

Then out of the blue you came home
unwell, you said, not you to moan
We called the Doc many times that week
soon a second opinion we had to seek

To hospital we went and just as well
for the scanner was there and it could tell
Deep down in your head was a nasty tumour
by now we had lost our sense of humour

We'll cut it out, the surgeon said
and quickly sent you off to bed
He dug most of it out with his JCB
but left the rest for radiotherapy

You were slipping away, I was very distressed
when a miracle happened and you were blessed
God's presence was there in that room that day
He guided you through to another day

From that time on you began to improve
no looking back, no headaches to soothe
We settled down to a different life
husband at home with caring wife

For nineteen months we shared this new style
with you by my side it was grand for a while
Then God decided your time had now come
and He took you away but I didn't feel numb

My prayers had been answered we had been given more time
my memories are treasures, of when you were mine.

Pamela Harrison-Haylett

A CHILD'S PRAYER

I'm a little girl in a children's home
All I want is a mum to call my own.

Some children are adopted, some find a foster mum.
I sit and wait and wonder, will my day ever come?

When people come to visit, they smile and say hello
But I'm not the little one who's with them when they go.

I think they choose the pretty ones, the others do not go
I wonder if I'm pretty, I really do not know.

I'll look into the mirror and see what face looks back
Perhaps I've found the reason - the face I see is black!

Now I know why I'm left here all alone
All I want is a mum to call my own.

Sonia Griffiths

WAYLAND

In his circle of trees on the Ridgeway
he shod his white horse and went away

Fire in his breath, hammer in hand:
dark master of iron from the womb of the land.

His laugh is windswept, vague is his hue;
but the earth rejoices at his craft ever new.

Now as the corn grows or cracks in the sun
or the gold in the leaves tells of autumn begun:

as the green springs in the lengthened daylight
or white lady moon lights the winter snows bright

Old Wayland goes riding or making alone
on his white horse of power by blood and bone.

Now as the land's crushed beneath concrete and cars
or forests are felled for the supermarket wars

or as the springs bleed and drain without tears
or new homes are needed and the river disappears.

Is Wayland on his horse, guarding his fire
or running on empty, burnt out of desire?

Paul Thompson

MY SON

Lord, you gave to me a special son,
So gentle, meek and mild.
A gift sent down from heaven
My precious little child
I loved him long, I shared with him
Fond memories to treasure.
A love so loyal, fond and true.
A love beyond all measure.
Through all the years, I watched him grow
I shared with him his touch,
He gave me so much joy in life
And things that meant so much.
I looked on him with so much pride
I never had a clue
You meant for him now as a man
To come back home to you.
And though at times, the loss of him
Tears my heart in two
I somehow find a comfort.
In knowing he's with you.
For Lord, you know the pain I feel
As I go from day to day
You sacrificed your *son* for us
So that we might find the way
The way to everlasting love
Sent down in spirit from above
Spirit to warm, and hearts to bless
Forever with your *holiness.*

Rita E Dilks

FAREWELL OLD FRIEND

In the twinkling of an eye
This body we do borrow,
There is no time for you and I
Before our next tomorrow.

Goodbye we say to all our tears
Tormented by your passing,
Going back on all the years
Of memories which are lasting.

There was more than just a few
Touched by your golden light
And it was because of you
They too are shining bright.

The sweetest music to our ears.
melodic voices ringing,
Will be hard for many years
In heaven now you are singing.

Jackie Coman

FORBIDDEN YOU

You dictate my every thought
All through the day and night
My head is filled with dreams of you
I know that it's not right.

You belong to someone else
How I wish that you were mine
My empty heart would be content
Until the end of time.

These thoughts I know I must resist
I try and try again.
My head says no my heart says yes
It's driving me insane.

I've never felt this way before
I don't know what to do
Can't think, can't sleep, it hurts inside
And it's all because of you.

Jon Baker

THE WHIST DRIVE

I go to whist drives every week
To meet my friends - a prize to seek.
The hands I get are often bad
Sometimes they make me feel quite mad!

Why is it, then, when trumps are hearts
I may discover the ace of hearts;
My partner leads out trumps to me
And her expression when she sees
I lead another suit instead!
And, golly, is my poor face red -
She takes the trick and leads it back
But once again I'm on the rack . . .
I have no master card to play
I'd like to go and hide away!
But when I'm also sure to get
The booby prize - you can surely bet
The last hand will be great - for then
I'm bound to finish with a ten!

Inez M Henson

A Story Of Exiled Love In An Oasis By Egypt's River Nile

Jesus plucks a lotus flower, and gives it to his mother,
Mary eyes its petals blue, but returns it to her lover -
'Wear the priestly blue yourself, as Melchisdech of old,
Sign of sacerdotal joy, and celestial praise untold.'

Jesus plucks a gilley flower, it is crimson purple bright,
Mary turns her eyes away, she cannot bear the sight . . .
Daren't recall prophetic words of sword piercing soulful loss;
'Hug tight this bloom saviour-child, 'tis symbolic of your cross.'

Jesus plucks a marigold, with a quick triumphant smile.
Mary thinks of patriarchs, of baby Moses in the Nile,
Of David's line of prophets, having halos (like the flower);
'Keep this crown my baby king, as an emblem of your power.

Leonard Jones

Florence

As I was in the park today
I met a lady from down my way.
Her face was kind, her thoughts were caring,
And with the animals
Her food she was sharing.
She past us by as she walked away
And stopped to pass the time of day.
It was the nicest day that I have had
For when it ended my heart grew sad,
For the lady had to return for tea.
A beautiful lady with hair like snow .
What pleasure today gave me,
She will never know.

Lynette Dunn

MY QUESTIONS NEED ANSWERS

You say you need time and space,
But your love for me you won't erase.
You say you will be back in about a week
But I need far more than just to hear you speak.

I watch the phone and I pray for it to ring
But I suppose you'll be busy, well you'll be doing something
Forgive me if I'm wrong, by saying what's to be said
But my questions need answers as I lie alone in my bed.

If you love someone, why leave them feeling blue,
You should stay by whom you love, unless the love is untrue.
So that's why I have my doubts, to why you won't return to me,
Because if your love was true, home is where you would be.

You say sorry for hurting me, so why continue the pain
Please come home to me and the kids, and please remain.
I will try to understand your problems, if you'd only share them with
me,
A problem shared is a problem halved, so please hurry home to me.

You're playing games with my heart, and it just isn't fair.
So please stop this hurting if you really care.
Let's be a proper family and share all our thoughts and fears.
Maybe only then will I stop this river of tears.

Sharon Allison

IF ONLY

If only yesterday were today,
and tomorrow had yet to come.
What changes would we make ,
were it granted to each and every one.
Would we grasp the opportunities,
that so often go astray.
To lend the more unfortunate
a hand along the way.

If only yesterday were today,
and tomorrow had yet to come.
Should we look more deeply
At the things we could have done.
Withdraw that sharp unfriendly
word, and to compromise.
We owe it to our fellow man to live
together, not antagonise.

If only yesterday was today
And tomorrow had yet to come.
Let's tackle poverty, greed and evil,
There's work that must be done.
And today is here to fill,
With those things we cannot shun.
Let's start that uphill climb,
Before tomorrow comes.

C Matthews

TIME LINES

Hiding behind the sepia
And the stiffness of the age,
My great-relations' hearts are yearning
To escape their Midland cage.

And in days they'll board for America,
Watching England slip to the waves,
As the Titanic forges westwards
And kills more than it saves.

They had their tickets in their hands,
Their luggage contained their homes,
They were a heartbeat's skip from leaving
To build their pleasure domes . . .

But a hand stretched out to touch them,
Turned their heads to the factory gates
And they felt their hearts were anchored
Bared their souls to history's fate.

And the ship went sailing on,
And Hollywood stole the mast
And my great-relations are absent
From the movie's mournful cast.

Ben Banyard

OUR MEG

The house is strangely silent,
The cats no longer roam,
They look at me with anxious eyes,
'Cos Meg is not at home.
They sit beside her empty bed,
Gazing at the door,
Waiting for their old pal Meg
To come and play once more.
I cannot make them understand
That Meg has passed away,
'She's in heaven with the angels,'
Is all that I can say.
We all love and miss her,
But, happy and free from pain,
We know she'll be there to greet us,
When we all meet again.

Mary Davies

THE LOVER

I understand you don't want to hurt her, but I've got feelings too,
My memories of our time together are ruined by my knowing of your
                                            deep down guilt.
Don't say one more time you love her, because how can that be true,
I'm the one you're lying here with, I'm the one you just made love to.
Don't say you love me, don't make it harder for me to let you go.
I'm trying to be cool to make it easier on you,
So when you leave to kiss her good morning, don't look back
Because I'll be stood at the window looking on. The cool front with you
                                            gone.
The heartbroken me stood in the morning sun's rays of reality, knowing
                                    that I've lost and she's won.

Emilie Clark

NIAGARA

The Horseshoe Falls of Canada are an awe inspiring sight
With masses of white water glistening in the light.
The huge white wall of water, rushing, crashing, swirling
Into foam and mist and spray, rushing from Lake Erie,
Down to Lake Ontario.
The Horseshoe Falls of Canada, are a wonder to behold,
Carved from the rock by glacier, when the land was bound in cold.
The swirling wall of water, crashing over precipice.
Dividing round Goat Island, this gem the waters miss,
Racing onward through the gorge,
Which forms a natural gate
Between the northern Canada,
And the United States.

Janet McKinney

TEARS OF A WILLOW

The willow by the rippling rill
Beyond the valley and o'er the hill
Weeps for arms like its boughs entwined
Moments for which it has long since pined
Arms which embraced in the rapture of love
Hearts at peace as the fantailed dove
Weep not for us oh willow green
Love such as ours has never been
The zephyr of my loved one's breath
Stirs your leaves though lost in death
Hark to his voice and listen well
He awaits for me in this wooded dell
Till my soul is free to roam at will
I'll come to you and the rippling rill.

Grace Johnson

WHEN LOVE DIES

When did you stop loving me,
Was it a long time ago,
I question why you've made me sad
Because I still love you so.
Can't you remember when we first met
The feelings that we had.
The thrill of meeting in our special places,
Then the partings which were so bad.
We have both got older together.
And we made vows, 'till death us do part,'
I know that feelings and love do alter
But darling you have broken my heart.
Is there nothing I can do to change your mind,
Just tell me what you want,
To live without you by my side
Is something that I can't.
I know you sigh whenever I ask
Are you going or will you stay,
Just put me out of this misery,
Although I dread what you will say.

Angela Butler

THE ART OF PIANO

Play that tune one, two three,
Play that tune just for me,
Let me see those fingers dance
Upon the keys I hear romance.
The tune plays on soft and low
With each note making music grow.

The pages turn one, two, three,
I admire the tune lovingly,
So sweet is the rhythm
Which it is givin'
So beautiful is the melody,
So beautiful, it is heavenly!

Julie Ann Doyle

DUN ROAMIN'

Moved house today. Never again!
No curtains for days and removal men!
How many cups of tea can you drink?

Should have moved before, but did not,
'Though we were first in the chain, we could not.
Everything packed bar the kitchen sink.

Working all hours. Ready to go.
Last minute panic. The agent said no,
Someone's pulled out. They've broken the link!

Solicitors bill came. Paid it.
The mortgage was arranged, so we signed it.
Too many empty accounts, I think!

Somehow we got here. The sun shone.
Each room chaotic. At last the men gone.
Beds have been made. I shan't sleep a wink.

Elizabeth Read

THEM UPSTAIRS

I don't ask very much from life
Now that I'm old and broke -
But why do neighbours seem to think
I'm such a decent bloke.

From 6 am to 10 pm
It's peaceful and so quiet -
From 10 pm to 3 am
You'd think there was a riot!

Then, car doors slam, the gate goes *bang*
And footsteps on the stair.
The dog next door joins in the noise -
I ask you, is it fair?

Keys in the door, doors slammed once more,
Then flushing of the loo -
Loud voices shouting overhead
With foul expletives too!

I really must remember
To stay up half the night -
Confront them in my *birthday suit*
And give them such a fright!

Brian M Wood

As Northampton Celebrated Its Balloon Festival, In August 1998

Up and away, in turn they go,
Swiftly climbing so very high,
Into an almost cloudless sky.
Balloons of different shapes and size,
Rising above all watchful eyes;
Now, higher still above the ground,
Into the silence all around -
Beyond the blaring noise below.

Soon, tiny shapes in God's vast sky.
O would such peace but permeate
The hearts of those, wherein lies hate
And bitterness, that is hell-bent,
With but one dastardly intent -
To destroy, kill, or badly maim
Life and limb of her or him -
Sometimes old, often young of age:
It matters not whatever stage
Of peaceful, joyous innocence;
Such needless carnage makes no sense -
But begs the question, 'Dear God, Why?'

Would that Ulster be blessed with such peace,
As from the basket of a balloon -
Not the destruction, death or injury,
As on one Saturday afternoon.
Let there be a permanent tribute,
Befitting all the injured, or dead:
That the treaty signed shall be agreed
That warring violence shall henceforth cease.

Glan Grey Jones

THE SKYLARK

The land lay in the golden haze
Of half-remembered childhood days,
And at the edge of memory
Where dreams play with reality
I thought I heard him come to me.

For as a child I loved to lie
Upon the grass to watch the sky
And feel his joy cascading down
To reach me lying on the ground
With arms outstretched to catch the sound.

And sitting on the hill to dream
Of all the things that might have been
And mourning golden days before;
I heard him rising, singing, soar
To touch the gate of heaven once more.

Catherine Reay

THE OLDEN DAYS

In the silence of my room when twilight falls
I sit and gaze at the pictures around the walls
A photograph of my dear Mum and Dad
Celebrating at their diamond wedding party for them we had

In the early days of our childhood
Life was not easy, they both worked hard to give us their best
Dad worked on the farm trudging for miles each day
With his horses and plough, no mechanical machinery and very low pay

Whilst Mum stood over a tub laundering people's linen
To help bring in an extra shilling
In their later years if a day out they took
A little gift was brought back we were never forgot

An ornamental wishing well was one I will always treasure
If it could make my wish come true, it would give me great pleasure
After all the years we have been apart
I still feel sad within my heart

Margery Day

THE SMART PARROT

Isn't it just amazing
What we can be trained to do!
But what you people don't realise,
Is that we're smarter than you,
You think that we don't understand,
What you're trying to say,
You think that you are teaching us,
Something new each day,
You reckon that you're smart,
When we begin to speak,
You think that you're so funny,
When we start to use our beaks,
Do you know how pathetic you sound,
When you repeat, 'Who's a pretty boy.'
You think that we're so grateful,
When you reward us with a toy,
We could tell you that we know,
And stop all of your fuss,
But watching humans act like fools,
Is too much fun for us.

Pamela Richardson

MUDDLED MIND

I just feel so despairing, what on earth am I to do
I cannot help but think that I could find another clue
I want to do it, no *I don't*, I'd like to run away
But if I did I know I'd have to tackle it some day
I may as well get stuck in and start the flamin' job
Instead of sitting fretting here, a useless feeble blob
Give me strength, I need to do so many other things
It wouldn't help me if I had more time, or angel's wings
Please help me out someone and give me some ideas
On what the best solution is regarding all my fears
They're growing out of all proportion and losing me much sleep
And more than that I'm frightened now that this could go too deep
If only I could talk myself into a better frame of mind
What am I saying, of course I can, I'm sure that I will find
A way through this by tuning into where I'd like to be
If not next month maybe a year or even two or three
But what is time when I am young and healthy, some call 'fit'
To do the things I want to do especially bit by bit
Just make a start and plod along until I get the feel
Of doing things methodically and then develop zeal
For what I see emerging as I trust my intuition
It should help begin to give to me a real sense of fruition
It won't be hard as I first thought to live in the positive
In fact it should be easier than remaining in the negative
The freedom and the choice I have are virtually unlimited
There won't be black and white involved, particularly primitive
The colours, feelings I envisage lift my spirits high
And surely it can stay that way from now until I die.

J Ireland

MY PRIDE AND JOY

There she stands outside my door
awaiting patiently
a rusting heap, of useless junk
but she belongs to me.

I bought her many years ago
when I was fairly poor
and get upset, when people laugh
and dogs wee up her door.

I would give her a re-spray
but that would be unjust
for any paint I put on her
won't match up with the rust.

I look at her with loving eyes
and full of ecstasy
then I get in behind the wheel
and drive off carefully.

I drive along the highway
at twenty miles an hour
she shakes and rolls, and bits drop off
and she aint got much power.

But I won't part with my old car
though all my friends agree
that she is just a heap of scrap
but she belongs to me.

Roy Turke

AFTERWARDS

As a passenger in a road traffic accident
Multiple fractures, plus a head injury meant
I was in a coma, so could not hear nor see
The doctors could not predict a future for me.

Lying in darkness, completely unaware
Had no worries did not have a care.
After ten long days, awoke at last
Memories were missing from my past.

Rotational vertigo was so unexpected
Also in my case, totally neglected.
It was quite scary to be in the midst
Of this unknown force I could not resist.

Lacy net curtains whirled with speed
This dizziness was terrifying indeed.
It was really impossible to walk at all.
If I did not keep still, was sure to fall.

Then, I was a young mother of four,
Now, am a grandmother of six, I adore.
Twenty years on, appreciate life more
Than I would have ever done before.

My enthusiasm for life has not diminished
Creative ideas are not yet near finished.
I look forward to each day's new dawn
So glad I survived - almost reborn.

Sylvia Davis

AN ODE TO RACHEL

Tea no longer quenched my thirst
But I drank and drank till I nearly burst,
Something's going wrong with me -
Water only - I can't drink tea.

As time passed by, it was made quite plain
That proud little stork was at it again.
Yes, there was to be a number four
Of that, I was really now quite sure.

A general announcement it had to be
For the children were now grown up you see,
My duties were such that it must be said
The workload I carried somehow must be shed.

A child at my age seemed quite daunting
And proved to be just a little exhausting,
Thoughts of getting back to the baby routine,
With nappies and bibs, and the broken night scene.

This new adventure was hard indeed,
But God gives strength in time of need,
So hand in hand with Him I go
To learn the lessons I needed to know.

He taught me how to persevere,
Our little one would soon be here,
A precious gift - a bundle of love
Sent from the Heavenly Father above.

Beryl Sigournay

TWO BRIGHT LIGHTS

Two bright lights, smoking rubber, and squeaking brakes, took my life
away.
A moment frozen in my mind, still-frame, rewind, replay.
The whites of the monster's eye, the smiling lips of chrome,
The grilled nostrils puffing steam, and the bellowing of horn.
I braced myself and held on tight, to preserve myself from harm.

Two bright lights, then one loud slam!
No time for preparation, no time to make a plan.
Adrenaline charged my veins, no time to fight or flee,
Perspiration seeped through every pore, and heart increased its beat,
Prayers found my trembling lips, with fastened eyes that forged crow's
feet,
I whispered, oh my God, why me?

Now I sit and gaze at passers-by and wonder where they go,
I daydream a lot and reminisce the life I had before.
No Saturday nights, no shopping spree, no running for the bus.
No wolf-whistles or looks of admiration, just pity and disgust.
I long to work, to run, to dance, to erase all of the pain,
But two bright lights took my life and I will never be the same.

Days are long and lonely, and nights are filled with fear,
Sacrum numb and flat from sitting in my chair.
Four walls are my companion, and pills are oh so dear.
Darkness hides the anguish but can't console the grief,
The bed is no longer welcoming, and I'm afraid to sleep.
As the two bright lights keep haunting me, denying me of peace.

D Walters

PRINCE AND SACRIFICE

Homeward bound with plunder from Troy
The Cretan lord was full of joy;
His ship lay low in rolling waves
With sail aloft and oared by slaves.
Blue-backed dolphins sported in play
And seemed to speed them on their way.
Then Boreas unleashed his might,
The sun was veiled from mortal sight,
A raging sea on beam-ends broke,
The king raised up his arms and spoke,
He vowed, if he was spared to live
And see his home, then he would give
To Poseidon, the ocean god,
The first live thing on native sod
That greeted him, whate'er it be;
The storm withdrew, calm was the sea.

Idomeneus, king of Crete,
Set foot on land to see and meet
Idamante, his only son,
And rued, straightway, what he had done.
Lissom and young, the boy's desire
Had been to greet his royal sire,
Now by fate, he was doomed to lie
On altar stone, naked, to die,
To give his blood by sunrise light
In ancient, sacrificial rite.
Aurora saw the thread of life,
Twelve years in span, cut by the knife.
Childhood's innocent heart was stilled,
The gods appeased, a vow fulfilled.

Ralph Smith

I WAS THERE

The night was dark and eerie,
The day now truly dead,
There didn't seem a soul about
Every one had gone to bed,
The street lamps here had all gone out
There was a stillness in the park,
When suddenly a rustling sound
Echoed in the dark,
I could hear the dried leaves crunch
As they were disturbed on the grass,
I stood there in the dark, transfixed,
As I felt 'the thing' go past
I'm sure my hair stood up on end
As I rummaged for my light,
I was wondering what it could be
As it disappeared into the night,
But before it finally vanished
It turned and looked my way,
I was wishing for a miracle
For the night to turn into day.
I was sure 'the thing' would get me
I was scared out of my socks,
But I breathed a sigh of great relief
When I saw 'the thing' was just a fox.

Barbara Ellison

THE TROUT STREAM

The dogwoods stand stiffly, their bark sunset shining,
The golden fringed willow, its fronds intertwining,
     Caresses the stream.
The water glides swiftly with crystalline flowing;
The trout swim in freedom, their silver scales glowing
     Aslant the sunbeam.

The lovers stroll gently, their mood sweetly pensive.
The fish 'neath their shadow become apprehensive,
     Aware of some harm.
He stoops; takes a pebble and carelessly throws it
At shapes dimly lit as they scatter. Of course it
     Must shatter their calm.

She turns to him sadly, her lucid eyes filling.
Retorts he, abruptly, 'It's better than killing
     And only for pleasure.'
'It's unkind, beloved,' and reaching to kiss him,
'A poor excuse hoping the stone's path will miss them,
     For they're nature's treasure.'

They make their way homeward across springtime places.
Time comforts the mirror and smoothes ruffled traces,
     Of thoughtlessness stain.
The swirl of mud settles; the fish glide in silence;
Returning, the purity overcomes violence
     And peace reigns again.

Janet Miller

CHRISTIAN THOUGHTS

If I can make a life a little brighter
By kindly word or deed, or friendly smile,
Or perhaps, to make a load a little lighter
By walking with a friend, that extra mile.

If I can turn a soul away from sorrow
And comfort them amid their grief and pain,
To let them know the sun will shine tomorrow,
For sunshine always follows, after rain.

If I can do my duty to another,
Just one good deed for each and every day,
To help a sister or an ailing brother
To walk in peace and faith on God's highway.

If I can keep my little candle burning,
And show the way to wanderers in distress,
To make a pathway brighter at each turning,
Bringing to each life, some happiness.

If I can help when all around seems dreary,
When every part of life is upside-down,
If I can keep on smiling and be cheery,
Bringing back that smile to end a frown.

If I can aim to be just like my Maker,
Giving to each day, my very best,
If I can be a giver not a taker,
Then I will feel that I am truly blessed.

Thomas Henry Hanson

THE ELUSIVE SPRITE

Hello, I think I hear the post,
I must be a reluctant host
The spirit does not come by day,
But just at night that it makes hay.

I seek him here, I seek him there,
Beneath the table, on a chair.
He flits around most anywhere.
Indulging in his trickery,
I think I've solved the mystery.

Just at dusk, he causes trouble,
My head is in an awful muddle.
If only I could catch and throttle
The sprite who lives inside the bottle.

Cynthia Briggs

EVERY POEM

I'm going to be a popstar
My dream job is to sing
I'll show the world how good I am
And do my funky thing.

I'm going to be a millionaire
No matter what you say
I know I can get to the top
I'll do it my own way

You can say whatever you like
I'll make it on Top of the Pops
I will carry on forever
Because the music never stops.

Tamsin King (11)

FORTUNE'S SMILE

We were fighting despair with economy fare and no treats or goodies or
cash for repairs.
Taxes and house bills dulled each waking day and our tiny cottage was
crumbling away.
Ben and Joseph needed some fun but clothing and shoes were costs
never done.
When passing a car park one drizzly day, wet, upon the ground they lay.
Two round pennies, small legal tender . . . a fortune, a sign . . . that
good luck meanders.
For two pence I buy one lolly sweet, with dimples and smiles, Joseph
sucks on his treat.
Jack came home tired from his menial tasks . . . overworked . . .
prospect less but employed at last.
Ben raced in from the lane nearby with a triumphant gleam in his eye.
'Look it's mine. . . I found it in a field' . . . hexagonal and hefty . . . fifty
pence was revealed.
The family raised celebrations with hot cups of tea . . . two finds of
money in one day . . . yippee!
Jack and I hoping our luck had changed, talked of the future and how
we could manage.
'Oh love . . . I forgot . . . it's on my bike in a bag . . . a man at the depot
gave me some rag,
old curtains from a boot sale somewhere . . . useful only for cleaning his
car'.
I dragged out the torn dusty brocade, with weighted hems so beautifully
made.
Idly, I unpicked a tight hem just to see what heavied the fabric so
purposely.
My heart thumped . . . I gasped . . . 'Jack look . . . quick' thirty weights
were in the hems - so thick.
'My God - it's a sovereign!' . . . stunned . . . we stacked the shining pile
. . . then as the tears came . . . we basked in fortune's smile.

Eve Mugford

AFTER THE STORM

It is early morning at first light,
Flat gold sand stretches wide.
Man's discarded rubbish swept away
By last night's angry outward tide.
Someone strolls the strand today,
Alone but for gulls' mournful song.
Dawn's pale light meets silver sea
Where brown sailed barges glide along.
Gracefully they move, sails unfurled,
For east coast sea is calm at last.
A gentle swell catches sun's first ray
And at water's edge little waves play -
Tranquil now after last night's storm.
But the sea's mighty, thunderous power
Terrifying, unforgettable memories form.
Howling wind raising huge dark waves.
Churning, splashing, creaming foam
Pounding angrily at manmade shore.
Timbered groynes creak and groan.
All nature's turbulent life is there,
Rampant, obedient to no power but one.
He who can quell all storms at will,
Has today ordained a peaceful morn.
He has called for early morning sun,
For those brave enough to rise at dawn.

Dorothy Harris

IRENE

I loved you. How could you not know and love me too.
Ours was that childhood romance
That sweet childhood innocent love
That you never gave a chance.

Why now do you torture me in dreams of your return.
Why now do you still enter my dreams Irene
Will you never learn.

Even then, it's with another in tow.
Even in my dreams you still don't know
How much I loved you, how pure my love
Was I that stupid, good God above.

It hurts to dream when you still don't care
But I loved you, and just to know you are there
Gives me hope that another time another place
I can hold you and love conquer whatever,
Whatever, at my own sweet pace.

I was young, yes I was shy, I wasn't stupid
No - not I.
Just pure innocent love, a marvellous thing
So marvellous I wish that everything
Could be so pure, could be so kind
I loved you girl - but never mind.

Now we are both old, and maybe you are dead
Maybe this poem will never be read
But I cry as I write, and feel such despair
Oh Rene - my love! if only you'd care.

When you next visit my dreams, make them
Sweetness and light.
When you visit again, let us be young, let's be bright.
Let us be smart, let us both play,
Let us be madly in love - from the very first day.

Roy William Brown

THE BLIND WOMAN

She sits forlorn within her world of darkness
And gently strokes the kitten on her knee
While listening to the music from the radio
Reminding her of days that used to be
Once more she's walking down the aisle to happiness
A vision dressed in gossamer and lace
She feels the ring he placed upon her finger
And sees again his handsome smiling face
Then the music changes to a lullaby
She holds within her arms a baby boy
Softly crooning her cup overflowing
She gazes down upon her pride and joy
Her life continues to unfold before her
Each precious moment she relives again
The music weaves for her a magic carpet
Blocking out all misery and pain
Alas now she is in her twilight years
Her men have perished fighting the good fight
And though she's blind she keeps them in her memory
And waits for them to lead her to the light.

Mary Dennis

El Cabrón (The Scamp)

Kirsty, I feel peckish, can we have a turkey for tea?
Yes Solomon, gladly will I serve thee.
With one swift motion the bird was caught
moments later, plush feathers he had naught
Licking his lips with relish the man thanked his fate
devoured his meal with vigour, cleaned his plate.
Two days later he moaned again
Knowing fully well that it would not be in vain
Kirsty, I feel peckish, can we have a turkey for tea?
Yes Solomon, gladly will I serve thee.
Anxious to please him she grabbed another bird
And throughout the village its plaintive cries could be heard
Six weeks had past and on sheer turkey he fed
By now the lonely widow was almost out of her head
The doctor had told him he'd had a bad heart
So for longevity, of lean meat he ought to take part
Stupendous tales of his journeys he did divulge
Promising foreign meanderings, exotic appetites soon to be indulged.
Concerned villagers began to whisper
Get rid of that craven man - he's a sponger!
But Solomon ruled by day and by night
Played mind games and gave her quite a fright.
At length and at last she looked out one morning
Just as the sun was laboriously dawning
In time to see him packed up and running.
Left alone and in much need of money
Now all she had was spent visions and a painful memory,
Surrounded by turkey feathers for company.

Helena Edwards Bishop

DIAMOND RING

I did buy a diamond ring
I knew you would sing.

With tears in your eyes
You said 'Thank you for the ring'
To you - it's everything
This diamond ring.

Third finger : left hand
That's where you placed the ring.

Then the surprise of your life
I want you for my wife
Let all our dreams come true
All I can say - is I love you!

Let me place a wedding band
On your third finger, left hand
Just say that you will
And it will be a thrill.

Just say the words
And I will wed you
I will place that wedding band
On your finger : left hand.

S McCourt

WATERWAYS OF THE TSARS

Waiting for a taxi which comes in time
Taking us to the coach, again in line
To wait quietly with the patient crowd
On holiday in the days allowed.

Hanging around the check-in was not bad
But once aboard the aircraft we were glad
To sit down in comfort for a few hours
Until, on landing, there are stately powers.

'Move over there! - queue here! And wait and wait
Until you're squeezed through the passport gate.
There are still bags to find and moves to the bus
Everyone follows making no fuss.

Arriving for our cruise we reach the river boat
'They're giving us the best they have,' they quote.

What shall we do with all the idle time
Raising a query on the meals they make
Walk the decks and see the world until we dine
As we sail it's so smooth through lochs and lakes.

Admire the towns and villages in the lanes
And see for ourselves how the folk must feel
As they invite us into their homes for gain
To raise their spirits and to make a deal.

They have our sympathy as well as dimes
We say 'hello' and 'thanks' and that's for real
Perhaps they see and know we share the pain
And more that can be done for their appeal.

For them rouble trouble needs a cure
It's experience for us and adventure.

Hugh Lincoln

APRIL FOOL

We got to thinking it was spring
Warmth surrounded every thing
The sun was out, no clouds in view
Around the corner flowers grew.

We really thought this must be spring
Buds all over opening
The birds were pairing up together
Embedding nests with down whatever.

So I donned a flouncy skirt
He now wore a stripey shirt
We went to walking through a wood
Linking arms feeling good.

Then Oh! a shower turned to rain
The wind blew forth and back again
Hailstones battered blouse and skirt
And blurred the stripes on stripey shirt.

Brealthlessly we stood and laughed
At two grown ups - looking daft
We should have thought of April's rules
For now she'd caught two April fools.

Elizabeth Jerome

FOR ANNE AND HARRY

Went to Penrith at the weekend
We took Anne and Harry through,
We went to see a place called Home
A cottage made for two.

It was a beautiful little cottage
With a garden all around,
Two up, two down, a job as well
Should suit them down to the ground.

Now Harry's got the gardener's job
And Anne's the typist too,
The money's good, the people swell,
They had the beds made up as well.

As you gaze out of their back door
Over the fields and through the trees
You can see through the hedge in the distance
The M6 motorway with ease.

And should you go out Penrith way
I'm sure they would like you to call
If you look for a place called Clathwaite
And look for Brackenhill Hall.

It's not very far along the lane,
It's cottage number three
And should you let them know you're going,
They'll have ready a pot of tea.

W I Horsfall

UNTITLED

I remember back in sixty-two
When I gave my love to you
It was all I could do
It was all I had to give to you.

We lived next door to each other on the avenue
That's the life we only knew
I was yours and you were mine
That's the life we knew.

We just wanted to rock and roll
Blue jeans and blue suede shoes that's all we knew,
We used to listen to the songs on the radio
I was yours and you were mine
And the time was fine.

Now Johnnie's in love with the girl next door
We don't rock and roll anymore
And Mary's down at the record store
For they don't want to be with us anymore
Golden oldies and we don't speak
We just run to a different beat.

It's so hard to understand
How we used to be
But time has passed on by
Now we don't seem to rock and roll anymore.

T M Ablett

Music Days!

Junior Band days were full of fun,
Now very much in the past,
And yet I've happy memories;
Laughter that will last!
Busy days spring to mind:
The concert; the contest!
And the Christmas celebrations
Weren't much of a rest!
One occasion I remember well:
Fellow players throwing a comb;
Which decided to do its worst;
Down *my* instrument to roam!
Rather hot under the collar,
I tried my best to smile,
And walked out onto the stage;
The comb resting in style!
There were panic-stricken moments,
Would the comb decide to rattle!
Especially on the solo parts,
But music overcame *that* battle!
Afterwards, I rescued the enemy,
And heaved a big sigh of relief!
And hoped the same group of lads
Would turn over a new leaf!

Denny Rhymer

THOMAS

Thomas our pussy cat went out hunting,
Down the street and past the bunting;
Because it was carnival day in our town,
This day when my story was written down.
He knew the way, for it is his habit
To see if he can chase a rabbit.
In the field by the Vicar's house
That is where he found the mouse.
He played about for an hour and a quarter
And even chased the mouse's daughter!
Then back he came, through the open door -
Placed the mouse on my kitchen floor!
Out in the town the parade was beginning.
The band started playing and people were singing.
The scene in my kitchen was equal delight
For any who did not share my fright.
I jumped on a stool and I screamed and I shouted
While hubby was wielding a stick, and he clouted
But missed the mouse, as it ran at a pace -
Thomas just sat there and washed his face.
Behind the cooker looked quite a good shelter,
So that's where the mouse ran, all helter-skelter.
I could not move to help at all,
'Twas hubby pulled the cooker away from the wall.
Then everything happened very speedily -
Cat pounced on mouse, then ate him up greedily.
Everything vanished except for a tail -
We thought we heard Thomas say 'I never fail.'

Janet Poundford

MEMORIES

The door is open just a crack
and gazing in, you can see the back
of an aged lady, in a rocking chair.
Her head is drooped, as though in prayer.
She's dreaming of schooldays, the friends that she had,
her days full of laughter, no time to be sad.
Of her sisters and brothers, not even a care,
the parties they had, the fun they did share.
The romances and dances that lovely blue gown,
the heartaches and heartbreaks, when her first love left town.
But later, she met and married her Dan,
a really truly handsome man.
But all these days have now long past
she has her dreams, and these will last.
Now her dog is with her night and day,
he is her friend, he leads her way.
He is her ears when someone calls,
he is there in case she slips and falls.
Soon the nurse will enter and tuck her in bed
but still the memories will go around in her head.

Coreen M Holmes

GOODBYE

The pain of loneliness
Too hard to bear
God save my soul
I don't belong anywhere.

The acquisition of stability
Comes from the trust that you find.
Lost memories, trying to resurface
Into your mind.

Fighting for inspiration,
Yearning to break free.
I want my sanity back,
I want me.

Love, a funny thing,
It makes you laugh, makes you cry.
For once I was happy,
Maybe that was a lie.

Now all I remember is a feeble goodbye.

Claudia Pereira-Mendoza

THE PATCHWORK QUILT

It used to lay on Gramma's bed,
Now it lies on mine.
It holds so many memories,
Long before my time.
Bright blue patches from a gown,
That hung behind a door.
Red, with little purple spots
Were from Gran's pinafore.
Green silk patches oh! so fine.
With roses, red and white,
Came from a very special gown,
Worn on her wedding night.
Stripes so bold, was once a shirt
That went with Grandad's hat.
He looked so fine and dandy,
In his photograph, like that,
This quilt tells me a story,
And each patch plays a part,
Of a time that's gone before me,
A precious work of art!

Mary Rose Samm

A BUS JOURNEY

'Please Father, show me the stop,' I said,
As I boarded a bus, to a place unknown.
I sat on the front seat, to look ahead,
Looking for a depot, in a strange town.

We travelled miles, then I saw a place,
A bus stop seen, that was right for me.
Alighting from the bus, in God's grace,
Trusting my Father, to take care of me.

I asked a youth, to show me the street,
But he declined, 'Stranger here' he said.
Next came an elderly lady, we did meet,
Asked her too, it's back there she said.

We returned the way my bus had driven,
To the garage where the old lady said.
Alas for me, the old lady was mistaken,
The depot she showed me was not named.

Next I asked a male grocer, I did meet,
Could he tell me where we should look.
He took me out, and showed me a street,
There at the bus stop, which I forsook.

Listening to others, could lead astray,
So listen to God, he will not fail you.
Only to the Father, should we all pray,
He is our Jesus, who wants to save you.

Fred Schofield

LIQUORICE ALLSORTS

In the last century a Mr Basset, a confectioner by trade,
Used to travel around, from shop to shop, carrying a large
Square white basket.

Inside the basket, carefully packed, in individual bags,
He carried his sweets, they were a rainbow of colours,
Each with a centre of black liquorice.

One dark winter morning, as he entered a shop, over the mat he did trip,
And horror of horrors, the basket turned upside down, and the sweets
Fell in a pile on the floor.

Mr Basset, a man of great distinction, kept a cool head
And said, 'In future, I will give my sweets a new name,
And call them *Liquorice Allsorts*.'

That is why today as you wonder around big stores or visit your
Small corner shop, you will see them displayed in all sorts of ways,
They say in Russia, they can't get enough of them.

I expect if the truth could only be told, the Queen has a packet
In her sideboard drawer, and when all this reigning gets
frightfully boring, she retires to her drawing-room, and there in
All her glory, tucks into her packet of *Liquorice Allsorts*.

So my advice to you dear friend, is that you visit your corner shop today
And there purchase two packets, yes two, not one,
Then visit a neighbour, or call on a friend, and together with the Queen,
Enjoy your *Liquorice Allsorts*.

Robert Warren

ROLE REVERSAL

'Don't worry, it will be OK.' she said encouragingly to me
As I set out upon my first day back at University.
'Have you got your pens, a ruler and your glasses?
And mind you take the timetable, you'll need it for the classes
There is no need to worry dear, it will work out fine,
Everyone is scared at first, improving over time.
You will not be on your own, there'll be others just like you,
Feeling strange and awkward, not knowing what to do.
The lectures are quite interesting, no time at all to shirk -
Concentrate, listen carefully, and industriously work
Towards the goal of passing. I will feel so proud
At the Awards Ceremony, when your name is read out loud.'
I had to smile secretly as I bid her fond Adieu -
She's the daughter, *I'm* the Mother - role reversal - *Déja vu!*

P R McDonald

THE MONEY MEN

There are no illusions left in life today
'Business is business, my boy' - they say.

Invest in a pension for the years ahead,
Become redundant and wait to be dead?

Life geared to money leaves no time for dreams,
Greed and self-aggrandisement is bursting at the seams.

Open the floodgates - let them all through,
But remember, the target is
                    You - You - and You!

D M Hawkes

THE FLEDGLING

As sleepy child needing rest
Lays its head on mother's breast,
So my soul sorely tried -
Fell from tree and sadly cried.
Here on Earth I can't survive
And need to soar where I can thrive.
A hungry cat is stalking me
And there is nowhere I can flee.
Lift me high, oh feathers mine
Return me to my cosy nest, where I,
In slumber can peacefully rest.
Launch this fledgling on maiden flight
And fill my heart with pure delight.
On outstretched wings enable me to fly
In joyous rapture beneath blue sky.

Audrey Luckhurst

YOU'RE AN INSIDE OUT PERSON

I'm an inside out person -
I came cocooned from inside out;
From my mother's warm womb
I arrived with a little shout.

A matrix created by an angel
like the interior of a church -
peaceful and protected in holy
waters we float and lurch.

My darling progenies, they're
inside out people too,
only when they were delivered
they weren't wearing a shoe!

Amita Chatterji

WORKING HORSES

Prehistoric man exploring in those times so long ago
Saw Epihippi quietly browsing, stopped and looked but did not know
That those strange creatures would develop and accept domestication.
Now we don't think it amazing to see horses gently grazing,
Changed from their origination.

With regret some people mourn the working horses' sad decline,
Now rarely seen as singles, powerful pairs or two's and three's in line,
Thrusting forward into collars, straps and links as taught as cables,
Bone and muscle, sinews straining, tributes to long hours of training.
Then to rest in quiet stables.

Machines replaced the working horses in the quest for more supplies,
Burning diesel fuel and sending noxious gases to the skies.
Efficiency and speed was all, but count the cost of the pollution.
Smoke and noise and dripping oil, contaminated air and soil.
An unwanted evolution.

In a Sussex Wealden setting in between the rolling downs,
Lie woodlands, slopes and verdant pastures close beside
                                        an old spa town.
People passing stop and look, wondering if there is more
Than meets the eye at that location, suggesting that perambulation
Will show what they are questing for.

Horses working. Heavy horses used to farm in old traditions,
Drawing aged implements and unimpeded by conditions
Weatherwise affecting tractors, turning earth to sticky clay,
Monster engines, exhausts roaring, multiple equipment drawing,
Shattering the tranquil day.

Horses working. Working horses stepping forth with surging power,
Toiling in a rural setting, plodding onward by the hour.
When fossil fuels are all but gone perhaps this countryside will see
Horse and handler, mutually trusting, passing broken tractors rusting.
Relics of what used to be.

J M Guerrier

THE DOWNS

I've walked these hills for many years
They've shared my hopes, my joy, my fears
On grass soft banks I've laid to ponder
What lies beyond the blue haze yonder

I've dreamt of days long since past
Of Stone Age man, his tombs deep grassed
The Romans bold once trod this way
With banners bright they came to stay

Then Vikings fierce with yellow hair
And helmets horned so proud did wear
Then Alfred came his Saxons bold
Were soon to break the Norseman's hold

The Roundheads and the Royalists came
The Downs were never quite the same
These green grass knolls saw many hanging
They heard gibbet chains gristly clanging

Peace then reigned for many a year
Till Hitler's war so filled with fear
The Downs were used as ranges then
Till the bells were heard in The Vale again

The sheep came by their bell a-ringing
Gentle shepherd lads more oft times singing
Passing by this way to country fairs
Disturbing rabbits, skylarks and hares

Maybe one day when we've passed by
There will be just earth, grass and sky
No more brash 'punks' with hair in spikes
Will break God's peace on motorbikes

Victor George Day

THE UNSUNG HERO

Upon the dizzy heights he stands, polishing the panes of glass;
Beneath him in the busy street heedlessly the people pass.
Scorning safety there is he
Hourly placed in jeopardy,
Yet the crowd is unaware
Of the hero working there.

He is a happy-hearted youth, healthy, venturesome and strong;
His thoughts are far away at home (he has not yet been wedded long).
When he's cleaned the final pane
He will travel home again.
Will he? Suddenly he's calling,
From the sill he's falling, falling.

At once the crowd is all concern. Can they comfort him or aid?
They see the ambulance arrive; he is on a stretcher laid.
Will he lose his useful life?
Who will tell his youthful wife?
Everyone is full of care
For the hero helpless there.

And so in every walk of life daily heroes come and go;
Of their trials, fears and triumphs no-one but themselves may know.
Unrecognised by they who pass
Thoughtlessly in moving mass;
Words of praise are rarely said
Until they are bruised or dead.

Mary Richardson

THE SEASONS OF THE YEAR

Spring

Delphinium and lupins bold,
what pretty petals to behold.
The poppy soon will show its flower,
thankful for the April shower.

Summer

To see and touch these gifts of Spring,
it really is a glorious thing,
then swiftly follow Summer blooms,
and Autumn with its own perfumes.

Autumn

In the Autumn leaves will fall,
red and bronze from trees so tall,
fading flowers from days gone by,
wilt and droop, finally to die.

Winter

After that the Winter hurries,
with mistletoe and holly berries.
Christmas trees - no flowers at all,
then frost and ice, and snow to fall.

Winter, Summer, Autumn, Spring,
each season is a lovely thing.
To see changes through the year,
every month holding memories clear.

Beryl Holroyd Fidler

AN AUTUMN DAY

A memory I shall treasure till the day I die
We walked through the woods my husband and I
The leaves that were once green
The earlier part of the year
Are now red and gold and will soon disappear
The silence and the peace and the love we share
I think in this life is beyond compare
We just strolled along in our own peaceful way
I look up to the Lord and truthfully say
Thank you God for this autumn day
This memory will forever stay
He talked of his youth and days long gone
The years have rolled by with memories to cling upon
I thank God for us being together
In this beautiful autumn weather
Then as the winter time draws near
We will say thank you Lord for another year.

Glenis Dando

REMEMBRANCE DAY!
(Dedicated to my brother David born 11.11.63)

Hustle and bustle upon the stair
Whispering voices that made us aware
That something was happening tonight in our house,
Though my sister and I stayed quiet as a mouse.

In the room next to ours, our mother cried out
That all was not well, we were left in no doubt.
We sat up in bed, unable to sleep
Determined our own lonely vigil to keep.

My thoughts travelled back to earlier that day,
And a service in church where a poppy wreath lay
In remembrance of those who fought long ago
And lay down their lives for the peace we now know.

A sound brought me back to the present again,
A sound full of hope, no longer of pain.
We held each other, my sister and I,
- We'd just heard our newborn brother cry!

Alice Penman (nee Hamill)

I MISS HIM SO

Though years have passed my heart still cries
No chance to say our last goodbyes
As wrenched was he from out the blue
Not just a father, best friend too
He nurtured me, he watched me grow
And taught me all I had to know
A caring man throughout my life
A saviour in my hours of strife
With virtues true he made me proud
A modest man, not brash or loud
He'd say 'Be kind and honest too'
As special men there are but few
There are many things that we should learn
Respect and trust we all must earn
And though he's gone I feel him near
My own demise I shall not fear
For he gave me life, he paved the way
I know we'll meet again one day

Yasmin Oakes

THE LOST SHEEP

He wandered along with scarcely a care,
Enjoying the freedom, the balmy fresh air;
Leaving the flock, the shepherd as well,
He gambolled along through each valley and dell.

No thought of the dangers that could lie ahead,
For a moment, had entered his woolly sheep's head.
He cared not at all for the rest of the sheep,
As they entered the fold and settled to sleep.

The night came quickly, it does in the East,
Scenery barren, no grass for a feast;
Cries of wild animals pierced the night sky,
No shepherd, no flock, no safety close by.

Back in the fold, sheep safe for the night,
The good shepherd thought of the little sheep's plight.
Probably frightened, hurt and alone,
He resolved to find him, and bring him straight home.

He left the flock in care of a friend,
He walked all night down track, around bend,
Then in the darkness he heard a weak cry,
Caught in a thicket, his lamb was close by.

He gathered him up in his strong shepherd's arms
Calming his fears, his many alarms;
On his broad shoulders he carried him home -
Safe and secure, no more to roam.

We too have a Shepherd who cares for His own,
But we are like sheep, and sometimes we roam.
Dear loving Shepherd, please keep us secure,
In Your arms enfolded, to wander no more.

Mary Studley

JUST THE TICKET

Jogging along on the seven-one-three
Over the Downs with a view to the sea
Passing the hikers all laden with packs
Braving the wind in their blue anoraks
Down to the Cuckmere and over the bridge
Climbing again to the top of the ridge
Rocking and rolling and on through the rain
If you want sunshine, then get off to Spain!
Past the Marina, the Windmill, the shops
Press on the bell now
And wait till it stops.
Here we are Brighton!
Ready for fun.
Wonderful Welcome
Here comes the sun!

Gwenda M Stanton

LAUGHTER IN THE RAIN

I'll never forget
      the laughter in the rain
I'll never forget walks down Lover's Lane
I'll never forget plans we made
      for the coming days
I'll never forget storms like raging seas
      that blow away with the winds
I'll never forget all the little things
      but most of all, I'll never forget
      the laughter in the rain
      to the sad farewell
      never to come again.

Brenda Walton

THE JOURNEY

I was born so far from my journey's source,
Carried by the winds on nature's course,
Far from the womb of my Mother the sea,
To rain upon the mountain scree.

And so begins my journey for home,
For now the miles and courses I'll roam.
On a falling and twisting switch-back ride,
Before I'll taste the incoming tide.

Pouring down through cranny and nook,
In a race to become a babbling brook.
Meeting others who join with me,
To escape our mountain's captivity.

I've followed this course since the dawn of time,
Following nature's contour line,
Sustaining the land so green and fertile,
Feeding mankind for mile after mile.

Rolling onward through fields and meadows,
Through green birch woods with leafy shadows,
Past herds of cattle and flocks of sheep,
My path remorseless, silent and deep.

Mankind has fished from my waters so clear,
With weirs and locks his boats he could steer,
From the coastal port to the farm in the hills,
Where I've watered his fields and powered his mills.

Such benefits I've given, yet received such abuse,
My waters now clouded from constant misuse
From unfiltered chemicals and effluent waste;
The bitterness of death is all I can taste.

And so to the sea I now return
My waters now black, my chemicals burn.
No welcoming smile from my Mother the sea,
For man has corrupted and altered me.

And now the cycle begins again,
But now I fall as acid rain.
I poison the land, and the land poisons me,
From this cycle of death we'll never be free.

K Roper

THE ROAD FORWARD

If the road to hell be paved at all,
then what of me? Temptation tall,
goading long and begging me,
lose yourself, appetite, see!
base and vile, you must admit,
gives us greed, for more of it,
to find the way, from grossness foul,
begin new life, slip off the cowl,
of envy's hate, resentful seed,
mourning time, of vicious creed,
wasting you, squandering hope,
remind us all that we shall cope,
and find intention, good or bad,
through hellish gate, passions sad,
before the end, a glimpse of light,
way up there the mountain's sight,
for us to see, through eyes of blind,
fading shadow, heaven's kind,
to rogues and thieves, suffer them,
a helping hand, knowing when,
smooth the way, and bring the sun,
for them to delve in pleasures won,
what a thing, glory's worn,
brings a life, in blinding dawn.

C Thornton

JOB-HUNTING

Married at 20, but carried on working
First child at 23 - planned and longed for
From my job, time for shirking.
Time for children - 1, 2 and then one more.

Secretarial work was my game
Now it was nappies, bottles and cleaning house.
I was my own boss, no-one else to blame,
I didn't mind - I had no grouse.

I love my children, but money was tight,
So I worked, doing whatever, wherever,
Cleaning, caring, chopping veg - so was my plight,
Anything to get the pennies - nothing too clever.

Back to college I had to go.
I needed updating.
No typewriters or carbon copies on show
Just computers and fax machines for communicating.

I passed my exams with a flourish
Preparing myself for the right time.
When I had to find the courage,
To start again whilst in my prime.

Now I am able to find a job,
The youngest at school since September.
However, all I get is a big fat fob,
Hey! I'm skilled, experienced, remember!

CVs sent, application forms returned,
Many Evening Telegraphs on a Thursday burned
Secretary, typist or even filing clerk.
Please let me have some work,

Still no replies, but I'll persevere,
I will get a job *this year!*

Jane Stupples

A Marriage Made In Heaven

My parents were born in nineteen hundred and seven
And I'd call it a marriage made in heaven.
It seemed certain that Mam would capture Dad's heart
For they were born only nine days apart.
Altogether, they had fifty-five years of happiness, laughter and tears.
Dad was not in the Army, but in the Home Guard.
But at that time, life was rather hard,
They lived near the station, there was a sign
Of war, when it was hit by a land mine,
And, faced by this horrific crime, Dad just got into the shelter in time,
But not before it had bruised his eye,
And though safe, he sat there and wondered why
Then finally at the end of the strife
They did embark on a happier life -
With me, their first child and later another
Was added - Fred, my baby brother.
Mam fell ill, and in nineteen eighty eight
She died, and Dad's sorrow was really great
Then, to finish the tale of a marriage so rare
He only lived for two years without her,
When I think of them, I can lesson the pain
By remembering that they are together again.
Now the street where I live is rather deserted,
But my loneliness can be averted
When I think of the couple who gave me birth,
Floating together above the earth,
And each time I recall them, and feel great pain
I remember their heaven-made marriage again.

Doreen Parsons

TALE OF A BLUE DRAGON

There once was a blue dragon,
It lived in the field of snows.
The people called it Rudolphus
Because it was blue except for its nose.

Its nose was red, the rest was blue,
Making it seem he had a cold,
Compared to the world he was young,
But to other things Rudolphus was old.

But he was a lonely dragon,
Of him everyone was afraid,
The King told them to stay away,
And of course, the people obeyed.

Now it came that there was a Princess,
And that she was lonely too,
They decided to explore together,
And so together off they flew.

They headed for the Place of Lore
A warm and lovely place,
No one knew if it existed,
So it was a good challenge to face.

They flew over the water,
Heading towards a new land,
And eventually they did see it,
And they landed on the sand.

And both dragon and Princess,
Chose to stay in the Place of Lore,
And the blue dragon Rudolphus,
Had a red nose no more.

Dominic McDermott

WOMEN'S WILES

A long time ago, as I've heard tell
Of a poor little lass, a simple gel
And of a mighty Queen, desiring to tease
Arranged an abduction, herself to please.
Whilst in the arms of Morpheus she lay
To the King's castle she was taken away
There in the heart of the King's great palace
Robed in silks and delicate lace
There presented to the handsome King
In golden crown and robes flowing
She did curtsey right gracefully
And bowed herself on bended knee
The King stood amazement in his eye
To light upon that child most pleasingly
'Twas not his Queen as he could well see
But a child of God and the deep country
The son by his father she there did see
His eyes fast closed from deep ennui
His eyelids open to espy a vision
A once in a lifetime's revelation
He stepped right down and lent his arm
Looked into her eyes so tender and warm
'I take this woman to be my wife
And cleave to her for the rest of my life.'
The King did scold his wayward wife
For thoughtlessly playing with a delicate life
But thanks be to God, the fates proved right
All's well that well ends as well it might.
The Prince and his lass lived most happily
With three handsome sons and lasses three
Lasses of natural grace and much beauty

Robert Catlin

JUST ONCE MORE

The final journey has begun
The carriage decked with lilies sweet
Sleek and black with nodding plumes
The horses walk into the street.

People bow their heads in turn
Respect for he who lies within
Most did not know in life the soul
Who journeys past and leaves no kin

As if they know the sadness there
The horses pass with measured tread
Many times they've walked this way
Many times and many dead

Not for them to plough the field
Pull Brewer's Dray or win a race
No glory over National fence
Life for theme's a slower pace

Even they must play a part
On and on till death awaits
No fame, no wealth - Just daily toil
Until they reach those final gates

The bells start to ring their knell
They pass in turn through Church gates wide
When suddenly a mighty yell
Stops horse and mourners in their stride

A shrouded figure then appears
Says do not be afraid of me
He jumps down through the carriage doors
I am still alive you see.

I've often thought how it would be
this final journey down the lane
The carriage, horses, lilies too
Yes! I will do it all again

Sheila May Elder

THE LONDON UNDERGROUND

An intricate web of destinations,
That is scattered over London Town.
With fares that are purely astronomical,
Causing Londoners and foreigners to frown.
Some connections are known as Circle,
Some as District, Piccadilly or Jubilee,
One can travel where anyone wants,
Like Oxford Street for a mad shopping spree.
The escalators are always busy,
Passengers' tickets are consumed by the machines,
A world full of chaos and confusion,
A description, that befits London's rush hour scenes.
The underground is full of millions of people,
Those who travel for pleasure or commute to work every single day,
It is a national and international arena,
Where individuals drift past each other on their way.
The underground is the definitive London landmark,
Without it the Capital would be lost,
However, it calls for improvement,
One should cherish it at whatever cost.

F Buliciri

BE THANKFUL

Don't feel downhearted because you are old
You are as young as you feel
Or so we are told
Forget the snow and icy blasts
That chill your bones
Now Autumn's past.
For Christmas time is very near
And Christmas carollers will appear
With lanterns shining in the night
They sing their carols
With all their might
So don't be a moaner
Be of good cheer
And thank the Lord
That you are still here!

E Cuff

EMERGENCY

In the darkness of the night
I sit and hear you racing through the night
Your siren going ten to the dozen
Letting everyone know you're on your way
Your light flashing so blue and so bright
For everyone to see
Telling that someone to hold on
'Cos you're on your way to help that someone live

Bonnie M Frier

ANY REGRETS?

Do the Angels above, hand out instructions or warnings, when
                                    choosing a daughter.
I'll write to the Lord, and advise that they oughta!
I'm a little different, or so I'm told,
My secrets do I now unfold?
My first love was a Champion, but his rage inside, compared to none.
I danced with the Devil - Not once, but twice!
If I could turn back time, would I still throw the dice?
All grown up, but still a child,
Yet do I yearn still, for the wild?
To all my kin, I lured much sorrow,
But my glee, my soul, my warmth, could they purchase or even borrow?
Any regrets!
Any regrets!
I think not
I thank the Lord for my little lot!

Helen Jones

AUTUMN STROLL

Autumn sheds her glowing colours with the falling leaves
Woody scents and berries can never fail to please
Squirrels rummaging in the hedgerow, then flying through the trees.

Along the stubble field a pheasant struts
Walking home with gentle sunlight on my face
Distant fields are misty, spider's webs like lace.

Quietly remembering walks we used to take together,
And wishing that once again you could walk beside me,
And share this heavenly place.

N J Brocks

THE EVENING'S GLOW

In the glow of evening my thoughts return to you and me,
to a yesterday when love was young, as only ours could be
just like the evening glow of twilight,
it fades into tomorrow's light,
nothing can give back the love of yesterday,
your arms, your hands, your loving smile to sit and talk awhile,
love was bright oh give me yesterday's evening glow with you.

I like to remember in the twilight holding you tight,
stars above singing our song of love,
young and bright feeling so right with you,
in the evening's hush at twilight stars above were happy as we,
when you held me, it felt so right I need you tonight.
But all I have is a memory, of a special time,
in the evening's glow of twilight with you.
Oh give me back yesterday's evening glow with you.

If I could have you back I would not wander from your side
our love was young and bright in the starlight of one special night,
in the twilight evening's glow one memory is very special,
a happy night we shared.
I need you tonight but all I have is a memory,
in the evening's glow how you talked, how you smiled,
arms tenderly holding me loving and tender
so sweetly to be held in.
Oh give me back yesterday's evening glow with you.

The Western Dreamer

WORDS

Can words say really what you feel?
Can they express what is in one's heart?
And does I love you mean the same as when it's spoken,
Or mend a heart when it's broken?
Can they? For if it is so then I'll try.
I've missed your smile, and the love in your eyes.
The sweet softness of your lips,
That when close to mine, are of the sweetest wine.
I've missed holding your hand with our fingers entwined,
And a gentle squeeze comes to mind.
Your hair that's so beautiful and black,
That flies in the wind when you toss your head back,
                              to enjoy a good laugh.
I've missed your caresses, your gentleness, your fury too,
But all these things are really one wonderful you.
Can words say or tell of the joy, the gladness you bring,
Or the love and the pride, when your song I sing?
Well can they?
Or how proud when side by side we go for a walk,
Or maybe just sit and talk.
Then if this is so, it is hard to find the words,
The right words to express what's on my mind
To extol the virtues of one so loving and kind,
My darling, really, can they?

Aubrey Henstock

THE ROSE

What flower is more lovely than a
sun-kissed rose?
Petals like soft velvet, from her branches
grows.
There was a special rose, long, long ago.
When Jesus died upon a cross, and from his
tears did flow
A gentle seedling, did from it flower,
It came to be born in Our Lord's last hour.
Joseph of Aramithea brought it to our
homeland,
He planted it in Glastonbury, as though it
was all planned.
It even flowered in wintertime, it was a
precious sight,
That lovely flower, the rose, grew with all its might.
And now that lovely rose. blooms throughout
our realm,
It blooms so magnificently with Jesus at the
helm.
And like that rose so precious, to Our Lord
Of Kings,
We are all God's roses, we are his own
seedlings.
He nurtures us from the cradle to the grave,
He died upon a wooden cross, our precious
souls to save.
So remember when you see a rose in your
garden fair,
Remember he made us and the gentle roses
there.

Sheila Chimes

JOURNEYING FORTH

We wish you well, the two of you
As on your way you go
We hope you have a lovely time
But we will miss you so.

With things to do and sights to see
The time will go so fast.
But we will all be waiting here
'til you come home at last.

Just take this chance to do the things
That you both want to do
And when your wandering days are o'er
We're here to welcome you.

Look after one another well
And when things go amiss
Just turn to one another with
A hug, a smile, a kiss.

May God protect and guard you both
And keep you in his care
He'll guide the path ahead of you
In answer to our prayer.

So off you fly aboard that 'plane
But when in foreign climes
Just stop and think of those you love
Somewhere, some place, sometimes.

Margaret A James

WHERE THERE'S MUCK

Emily Mary Golthorpe, a scullery maid was she,
She said *goodbye* to Mother and all the family,
She trudged along the country lane, she didn't want to go,
The very thought of leaving home filled her full of woe,
She saw the big house yonder, she dreaded all the work,
Black leading grates and lighting fires, there was no time to shirk,
Her bedroom in the attic, was very cold and bare,
The big bed in the middle, with two she had to share,
Each morning she was wakened, the time was five o'clock,
To bathe with freezing water, was really quite a shock,
Emily Mary Golthorpe worked very hard indeed,
Her conscientiousness paid off, in her work she did succeed,
She became the parlour maid, the sewing maid, the cook,
She became the housekeeper, then she wrote a book,
Emily Mary Golthorpe, is very rich today,
She wrote about her working life, and really made it pay.

Jean Burch

YOU CAN'T ALWAYS GET WHAT YOU WANT

Your life is like a butterfly,
Never free from hassle.
Your beauty inside
Makes my life worthwhile.

You were so wild,
And now are mild.
You are not blind
But why are you so kind?

You are always there,
But I never dare
Because I care
I'd never per.

I love what is pure
And what must be endured.
I love the morning dew
And they who dare.

Andrea McLoughlin

SMALL IS BEAUTIFUL

Why is a woman so afraid
Of this small creature so well made
Why does she jump upon a chair
And sense the straightening of her hair?
The horror - that in her clean house
She should encounter this - a mouse!
So agile, quick, so very neat
The mouse manoeuvres round her feet
Making sure there is no cat
Feigning sleep upon the mat
Then stops to clean his whiskers fine
His soft-brown body all a-shine.
Tiny paws like dainty lace
Deftly clean his ears and face.
He stops and listens - time to think
Then climbs up to the kitchen sink
Nothing there- down to the floor
And over to the pantry door
Glances back, sees trembling there
The woman, still upon the chair!

Jennifer Huber

MEMORIES

How quick the span of life does pass
An aged parent from a little lass
Looking back over the years
Happy memories out number the tears

A child at school, oh how free!
Summer holidays by the sea
Before I reached twenty came the war
Blackened out windows shelters galore

I joined the girls in airforce blue
My bit for England I did do
I met my man became a bride
Once more in England peace did abide

A little house, a garden plot
Then arrived our first little tot
Then a brother and sister making three
Such happy days ahead of me

Fishing, camping, laughter tears,
Bedtime stories, ghostly fears
School behind them they had their skill
Each one struggling up the hill

They travelled far, they travelled wide
And took what came within their stride
Now all gone their separate ways
I live with memories of the golden days

Emily Margaret Rose

RAIN CAPE

In India's sunny clime
It wasn't sunny all the time
And when it rained -
. . . It rained.

My army service monsoon cape,
Hardly the fashion norm,
Voluminous and dun,
Braved many a drenching storm.

I wore it on Darjeeling's hills,
One downpour of a day,
Riding a care-worn pony,
Past Buddhists' flags agley.

Fifty years on in Dorset fair
At back of car it lies serene,
Until besmirched by muddy dogs,
Slumbering in doggy dream.

It can be worn in dire need,
When wintry gales provoke,
Mud-streaked and billowing in the wind,
A strangely mediaeval cloak.

Such noble end methinks, dog-stained,
Plangent with memories, new and old,
Recalling all those country walks
. . . And so much rain . . .

Anthony Bugler

IVY KEAY ON YOUR RETIREMENT

No more eggs and bacon
No more coffee pots
No more grills of scrambled eggs
For Charles to drop the lot

No more kipper fillets
No more cold York ham
No more grilled tomatoes
Or little pots of jam

No more filling milk jugs
No more Earl Grey tea
No more sticky marmalade
For the man on table three

No more prunes or All Bran
No more Weetabix
No more halves of grapefruit
For the guests on table six

No more clocking in or out
No more weekly pay
Now you've got your pension book
To help you pay your way

No more early rising
To get to work on time
No more trays to set in place
For our break at half past nine

No more laying up to do
For Trafalgar Tours
No more fumbling with the keys
To open Nigel's stores

Now you've reached retirement
And your working life is through
I'd like to say dear Ivy
It's been a pleasure knowing you.

Decima Irene Watkins

DAYS GONE BY

As a train went hissing by
I caught in the corner of my eye,
Beyond the doors of glass and steel
The graceful movement of the engine's wheels.
The whistle shrill the steam like molten dust
The tracks sparkled in light not an inkling of rust.
There were happy children glad to be there
On their Sunday School trip to the beach and the fair,
Where they could laugh and play and sing,
With Punch and Judy in full swing
And old box kites on a piece of string,
Where donkeys trotted on the shore
And salt sea air filled every pore
And fishing boats bobbed in and out
With their catches of lobster, mackerel and trout.
As I awoke and I don't lie,
Out of the corner of my eye,
There were Formica tables where wood had been,
It really was a different scene.
A tannoy message came across the air,
My destination, I was there.
As commuters rushed for every door
The tranquillity of days gone by was no more.

Gareth Thomas

DESERT SANDS

Take a look at the vast shifting desert sand
Soft and warm to the touch of the hand
Running slowly through your fingers to the ground
Nothing but sand, sand all around

Innocent to look at in its dunes
But when the winds come it plays other tunes
Small whirlwinds leave a trail where they have been
Sweeping across the desert like a clip from a cartoon scene

Then comes the sand storms from nowhere torn
Now is the time you wish you were never born
You can cover your face but you can never hide
The sand will search and uncover your pride

Flies by the millions there be
Ready to make a chameleon's tea
Their long tongues they flick out
That's another fly up the spout

Scorpions, praying mantis, sand asps as well
Live their lives in this dry hell
Pyards?, desert rats and gazelles search the barren waste
To find food, but in the heat of the day there's no haste

Sunrise, sunset is time like a clock
At night the temperature drop will crack a rock
The days are long, hot and dry
Nights, cold, quiet except for an animal cry

The ship of the desert it floats by
On the camel you sit up high
This creature with a hump can be vile
Treat it with respect and keep away from its bile

Arabs that live in the desert
To strangers can be very pleasant
Respect their customs and ways they will be a friend
Cross them and your life will end

The things I'll remember most about this land
Is being out in the sea of sand
And having the feeling of being lost
Than god for a compass and all it cost

Farewell to this land of hell
For me it left this poem to tell
A sight I would not have wanted to miss
But now I'm content in my home of peaceful bliss.

P Clark

FIRST VISIT TO CANADA

I remember the day you took me so high
In the building that seemed to reach to the sky.
A tiny church, green grass around
Coloured cars in the parking ground
All so small from where I stand
I felt I could hold them in my hand.
Then we had to turn away
For me the memory will always stay.
I wonder now, are you still floating high
In the building that seemed to reach to the sky.
Or in your new work have you found
Your feet are firmly on the ground.

Edie Scrivner

SORCERER

Searching for vengeance for a big injustice
Several times in the past he's always had the rough edge
From the man in the tower with the flashing magics
Who's gonna rule all the world with his wonderful ethics

Black magic and potions a really weird notion
The only way to live when the people think you're joking
'Just follow me and I'll make you all see
That the mysteries of the universe are found in you and me'

The crystal ball is glowing what is it showing?
Elements of surprise regurgitated knowing
Scenes from the past flashing back to back
Scenes from the future premeditated caricature

Falling off the world is his only escape
From the madness he feels and all his mistakes
See the stars shine in his eyes light up with surprise
When a magical potion causes immense devotion

And the people stand in awe in this small little town

'You can't escape from me I'm your destiny'
Its the sorcerer look he'll cast a spell or three
With the bell and the book a wicked charm a laugh
Is he real or a farce?

Trak

BLACKBIRD IN THE APPLE TREE

Blackbird in the apple tree
What is there to sing about
This wet and windy day
Singing just as sweetly
As in sunshine yesterday
Are you thanking God above
For sun and rain, the winds that blow
All things that grow

Or is it a lullaby
For the nestlings down below
Lulling to sleep the hungry ones
Who keep you busy all day

Now it could be a love song
To the lady perched close by her nest
Listening to every word
As she takes a well earned rest

I wish I knew what you are saying
I only know you lift my heart
As from your stage the apple tree
You thrill and throb, with little pause
The blossoms are a bouquet
The wind sounds like applause.

Owen Murphey

THE OLD PLUM TREE

There was an old plum tree
In a garden beside a country lane
Hanging over a wall loaded with plums to see
A miner going to work, spied this lovely sight
Temptation was too much for him
On this tree he did alight
For his snap-tin he did pick a few
In the early morning dew.

In the coal mine having his break
He called to his mate to have a plum
Among all that clinging black coal dust
So much enjoyed, the juice ran down
His mate asked, 'Where were these plums found?'
When he told him, amazed and angry
Said, 'Do you know, you picked my brother Sam's plums.'
'Oh Lord!' he said, 'I didn't know.
For I would have passed them by
The temptation was too great
When they just caught my eye.'

Well if our brother Sam had seen you,
I know what he would have said,
Come brother, come and get some,
From this tree the old Victoria Plum.'

Maud Sales

A MOTHER'S DREAM

My son's bedroom is tidy,
I can't believe my eyes.
I open the door, the mess is gone
And what? A lovely surprise?
The aftershave gel and socks have gone,
You can see the carpet once more.
There's no piles of dirty underwear
Strewn liberally across the floor.
The ironing takes me half the time,
The clothes horse has lost its sag,
No more hundred decibel music,
And I'm no longer called a nag.
I can even go to sleep at night,
Don't have to listen for his car.
The dog sleeps in his basket,
The hall doors not left ajar.
So is this then every mother's dream?
Do I have the perfect son?
No, the bed is no longer slept in,
It's to University he's gone.
And now I wish the mess was back,
I lay awake and listen for his car,
The dog sleeps by the hall door
In the hope it's been left ajar.
How long is it to Christmas?
When I know that he'll be home.
I really don't care about mess and noise,
And he can live on the goddam phone!

Janet De'Ath

THE GOOD SHEPHERD

The fold had settled for the night.
The sheep so snug and warm,
Seemed happy and contented,
Secure from wind and storm.
And yet the shepherd was aware
One of his charges was not there.

He made his count, but could not find
This single missing sheep,
And knew that he must once again
Dismiss all thoughts of sleep,
And face the weather, wet and cold
To bring his sheep back to the fold.

He knew that he would have to search
Mountain, and moor, and field.
These thoughts did not deter him,
He was their only shield.
Their only hope, their only friend,
On him alone they could depend.

After what seemed an endless search,
His efforts were repaid.
So happy was the shepherd,
In gratitude he prayed.
And stooped and lifted from the ground
The precious one that he had found.

He made his way back to the fold,
His loved one in his arms,
Never again to wander off
Now safe from all alarms.
In memory these words we keep,
'Rejoice, for I have found my sheep.'

Gordon J Tellam

BLIND FAITH

If there really is a God
Why did he create Ken Dodd?
If the Great One does exist
Why was George Best always pissed?
Why the killings, why the sin,
Why does Jimmy White not win?
If indeed, there is a God
Why could he not give the nod
And suffering would disappear
Sure every pub would have free beer.
The Man could make our lives a treat
Even Tebbitt would be sweet
No more wars, we'd live in peace
And best of all
No more 'Grease'!
Did you ever stop and think
What Almighty likes to drink
A Guinness or a Babycham?
I bet he likes an Irish dram.
If there really is a God
Don't you think he finds it odd
That Dolce got to number one
And lunatics can buy a gun
That Cliff still has a middle shade
And that he never once got laid
And so my friends we just don't know
What's in the sky or down below
We struggle on as best we can
'Cause that's the Father's master plan.

Gerard McAvoy

MATINEE

Aspiring stars
They have their dreams
And they have their
Faux pas too
They have their applause
Take their curtain calls too
And get interviewed
By BBC 2

They take their scripts
And learn their lines
Perfect their stage
Instructions . . .
Dimming the lights
On the partisan play and . . .
Firing the cast
At the thought of it.

Curtains rise
And curtains fall
The actors likewise too
One day in lights
The next in mud
But ultimately
Drained of blood.

The kids
In their silk pyjamas
Crying for a mummy and daddy
To love them
And do not think any less
Of their stinking attitude.

I mean
After all
The parents weren't there

When it counted
Just another stage set mounted . . .
Another wad of crisp bills counted . . .
Sad it should turn out this way . . .
Life . . . is just another matinee . . .

Sally Wyatt

TIME

They say time is a wonderful healer,
Time can be a good friend,
But what is the use of an ally,
When there is nothing left at the end.

What is the point of dreaming
Of holidays, future and plans
When you know the only thing you are sure of,
You will be left with just time on your hands.

People say, 'Go on, forget it,
Get out and start a life anew.'
The problem I have at the moment is,
It's something I don't want to do.

I don't want to forget my life's history,
I don't want to forget days gone by,
But one thing I know that's for certain,
I can't just sit here and cry.

I must get rid of depression,
Must regain self-respect and my pride,
Then perhaps I will really acknowledge,
It is good to have time on my side.

M C Luker

BLINDNESS OF A CHILD

Can you imagine a life forlorn,
'There are no words that I can form'

A child's eyes - that see no light;
'She cannot see the moonshine bright'

She cannot see the sunshine;
'Or the colour of a rose'

She cannot see the dewdrops;
'God's petals doth enfold'

She cannot see the snowdrop;
'Or the tulips - in the spring '

She cannot see our oceans,
'Or fledglings on the wing'

She can, however, feel the sunshine,
'And the breeze upon her face'

She also feels the icy breeze,
'And snowflakes - God doth make'

She also feels - her loved ones,
'And all their love embrace'

She also hears the morning lark;
'Who sings his morning song'

She also feels - our Lord's true faith;
'And knows where she belongs'

She may not have eyes that see;
'But she alone - beholds'

Nature's sounds about her still;
'Like God's petals enfold a rose'

Knowing she is loved by all;
'Our creator for her enfolds . . .'

Valerian Poems

MONGREL

They came again today and gave me scarce a glance.
They came again today; I knew I had no chance.
And as they wandered slowly arm in arm
They passed me by - a mongrel with no charm.

I'm old you see, and know there's little hope.
I'm old you see, and know they couldn't cope
With such as I, whose future now is bleak.
They passed me by - for I'm not what they seek.

Were I a puppy or some classic breed
Were I a puppy they would surely heed
My plaintive cry to find a home, and yet
They passed me by, with no word of regret.

I know I could be happy, and could make them happy too.
I know I could be happy, but my chances are too few.
There's nothing in the way I look that's pleasing to the eye.
They passed me by and wandered on, I know the reason why.

They came again today, but passed post haste.
They came again today, no time to waste.
I'm left to dream of things that cannot be,
They passed me by, as though they could not see.

S Cannan

STORY OF LOVE

Awesome and gentle,
Daft and sentimental -
I feel myself falling apart!
This being just hit my soul,
Simply, I lost control;
Feeling drunk to the depths of my heart!

Words never can explain
Just what happened to my brain
After the meeting took place
Blinded, I think, by lust -
Then given up to trust;
Inevitably, love's compliment will face.

For love, sweet, it will ignore
Any big or little flaw,
So long as it still can delude
Why, when we realise,
Do we choose to close our eyes,
Refusing to let reality intrude?

The moment we do pretend,
Leads to the unhappy end
Of watching things disintegrate.
Soft words no longer spoken,
My heart, I fear, is broken;
Love, the complexity I never did appreciate.

Love is the letting go,
When all other instincts beg for 'no' -
The hugs and the kisses are through
Love - once was everything,
Now it's not anything -
Melted down ,just as fast as it grew.

Sophie Allinson

THE TOOTH

Today young William wears a frown. I wonder what's amiss?
It's not like him to lose his smile and stamp about like this.
I'll ask him what the trouble is. He says he's got toothache.
It started hurting yesterday, all night he's been awake.
'Come on, young William,' mother says, 'to the dentist we will go.'
But Will draws back and shakes his head, 'To the dentist? No, no no!'
He cries and shouts but mother says, 'Now on that chair you sit!
The dentist is a kindly man. He won't hurt you a bit.
I'll phone to ask him when to come so there won't be long to wait.
Then we may come at ten o'clock? Oh good! We won't be late.'

Came half-past nine and time to go, but where was poor sad Will?
No sign of him upstairs or down - the house was very still.
Then out into the garden went William's mother kind.
She wondered where her son could be, hoped he'd not take long to find.
To the bottom of the garden she crept with softened tread,
Saw William in the apple tree, from his mouth there hung a thread.
He'd tied the end to a nearby branch and with his eyes shut tight
He tried to find the nerve to jump - but he felt too full of fright.
His mother smiled. She soon would solve poor William's difficulty.
As loudly as she could she shouted, 'William! Come down at once to
me!'

Poor William jumped before he'd thought, her voice surprised him so.
'And how's the tooth?' his mother asked, her voice now sweet and low.
He gave a wide and gappy grin, the tooth had gone 'twas clear.
He pointed up above his head. His tooth was hanging there.
'Well, there's a clever boy I have,' said Mother smiling still.
'There's no need now for the dentist's care with a boy so brave as
                                                        Will!'

M E Ficken

SASHA

A beautiful black Lab with velvet ears
At two years old we'd got years and years
Unwanted she came to live in our home
Never again did she want to roam

Serenity and calmness she brought along
Gentle and loving just like a song
Her neck stretched out upon my knee
How wise the eyes that looked at me

We walked together as if hand in hand
All my emotions she'd understand
She loved to swim and frolic in snow
Only four years with us we had to let her go

We needed to help her into the light
Leukaemia struck with all its might
Coat still glossy eyes still bright
She looked at me with love not fright

The day after you'd gone I picked flowers for you
I put them in a vase and said Sasha these are for you
When I returned home I smiled to see
Somehow she'd left one for me

She's been back to me healed and restored
God bless you Sash you're still adored
The thanks she gave helped me to see
Our animals live on as well as we.

Patricia Mackie

SMUGGLERS' GOLD

Out from the smugglers' cave he came
Spume-curled hair and eyes a-flame.
'I'll give you silks that have come from France,
Golden shoes that will make you dance.
Rings and bracelets for skin so fair,
If a smuggler's life on the sea you'll share.'

'Rings and necklets become me ill;
Of men's false speeches I've had my fill.
What do I want on your lawless barque,
The only girl among smugglers dark
And evil, tho' handsome too!
I'm spoken for, and it's not to you!'

'Oh yes, fair maid, indeed I know,
Spoken for Jim in the fields below,
A shepherd of lambs. More lambs there'll be
If you marry him now in your youth,' said he.
'Old you'll grow, though young be your years,
Hard-worked and punished and days full of tears.

A gentleman I, though smuggler too,
More than a shepherd can I give you.'
I twisted and turned and fled down the strand;
My arm was sore from the grasp of his hand.
He did not follow, but stood there, still,
Watching me climb the grassy hill.

I've wondered times as the years have passed,
What life would have carried before the mast;
Silks and satins bound in by the sea -
No green hills there to run and be free.
And I look at my bairns and I look at my man -
And I know I did right on the day I ran.

Elizabeth Morris

THE GARDEN SHED

There's a shed at the bottom of my garden
It stand there so sombre and grey
But strong and sturdy and mysterious
Filled with memories of yesterday.

It belonged to some neighbours of ours
Some thirty years ago
They departed these shores for a new life
In Australia, like so many who went before

I wonder what became of them
And if they wonder about us here
Could they but know how well that shed
Has served us through the years

Now alas it is so little used
It is sad to have to say
But still it stands defiant and bold
Ready to share in another day

The tools that served us so well in the past
Though blunt and rusty by years of neglect
Will be cleaned and sharpened by people who care
To be used by our friends I know not where

Who knows what pleasure those tools will bring
To the people who need a helping hand
But the shed in my garden will always be there
A reminder of the need to care and to share

Eva A Perrin

SPRING IS HERE

How wonderful to see the spring return,
Flowering almond trees have no concern
Of all the traffic passing by,
Their flowers held like pink clouds on high.

People drive around too fast,
Missing their beauty which will not last,
I wonder how many people see,
Their loveliness, or is it just me.

When I take my love to work,
I can't help but take a look,
At all the beauty of spring flowers,
If I had the time I could spend hours.

Travelling around to see them all,
From polyanthus to trees so tall,
There are golden daffodils as I drive past,
How I wish the spring could last.

Forsythia in hedges makes a splash,
All shades of yellow that never clash,
So find the time to stop and stare,
Before too long they won't be there.

Gone away until next spring
When once more their beauty they will bring.

Beryl Simmons

A MINOR STROKE

That day was just as ordinary as could be,
And we never thought it would end like this did we?
We had been out for the daily drive in our car,
Not into town, but visited our daughter, not far.
I noticed you seemed awkward handling tea cups,
But I did not worry about it all that much.
After lunch there was a big problem when you spoke,
Obvious then that you had had a minor stroke.
Since that time you have been extremely weak,
And suffer problems whenever you try to speak.
But other smaller problems have now got much better,
You can drive once more and manage to write letters.
Now you look well and people think it a huge joke,
When they ask about you, I say you had a stroke.

Susan Mullinger

GONE

Looking in the face of fear
Seeing why you're really here
The planets spin around your head
But you can't spend your life in bed
It won't be like it was before
Your dreams are knocking on the door.

You try to hold on to their hands
You're feeling yourself fade
It hurts so much that you must leave.
The friends that you have made.

Your mind shuts down, your soul is stirred
It's now time to move on
You wake up in a different place and everybody's gone.

The rain falls on the gravestones
That are standing all around
Now you must walk in to the light
For that's where you are bound.

Carl A Dignan

WALTER, THE UNIQUE SWEEP

Climbing up the ladder, to the highest rung,
Everyone is so surprised,
When they see what's being done.
It's Walter sweeping the chimney,
As happy as can be,
Pushing all the soot and dirt,
Down to poor old me.
But I don't mind the dirt and grime,
I tackle it with glee,
As the ladder I could never climb,
It's far too high for me.
From bottom to top there's lots of stress,
And also an awful amount of mess.
So there is only one way left to do,
And Walter gets a lovely view.

Dorothy Mezaks

THE STORY OF ZACCHAEUS

When Zacchaeus heard Jesus was coming to town,
he was very excited and jumped up and down:
he'd heard that Jesus was a very good man
who made people better and had many a fan.
So when Jesus appeared at the end of the street,
Zacchaeus was first to jump to his feet!
But in the crowds, because he wasn't tall
He found he couldn't see Jesus at all!
So eagerly he climbed up a nearby tree,
and peered through the branches the better to see;
but he couldn't believe it, as Jesus passed by,
He stopped, looked up and caught his eye!
'Hello Zacchaeus! - I'm glad you came.'
Zacchaeus gasped, 'How did you know my name?'
Jesus smiled, 'I know all about you, my friend -
can I come to your house at my journey's end?'
Zacchaeus nearly fell from the tree - he was thrilled -
but then with fear and dread he was filled;
for although he was very rich, he felt sad
because to get money, he'd been very bad.
'But nobody likes *me*, - I'm *nobody's* friend -
with somebody *better* your time you should spend!'
'Oh no!' said Jesus, 'I want to meet *you*,
and share a meal and a cup of tea too!'
So off they went home and talked as they ate,
and when Jesus left, it was getting quite late.
Zacchaeus never saw his new friend again,
but from that day on he was never the same,
for Jesus had changed him in every part,
and healed all the bad in his life and heart.

Helen M Seeley

HAPPINESS

Just a few simple words in rhyme
I think I'll manage in time.

Although my brain feels dead
And there's nothing in my head.

Perhaps I'll see the light
In the middle of the night.

It won't be romantic, it won't be blue
I must tell someone or this day I'll rue.

When once upon a time
In our swimming club fine.

Fred hurried by with his hand on his bot
Shouting, 'My trunks have split, so this is my lot.'

Jean lost her teeth and there they lay
Smiling in the pool like the buds in May.

There was Jim, George, Fred and Tim
Also Ivy, Hilda, Margaret and Kim.

Many more swimmers than this we had
During winter people thought we were mad.

When walking through Woolworths one day
I saw Fred coming my way.

I gave him a smile, but he didn't seem to know
I tried again but he looked quite low.

Then his face lit up, realisation for Fred
'I didn't know you with your clothes on' he said.

All seemed to hear him, was my face red
So I put a move on and raced after Fred.

Ivy Firth

ENGLAND MY ENGLAND

There will always be an England
That's the place where I was born
Where Mother Nature spread her beauty
With fields of golden corn
We have the tall trees in the meadow
Where the song birds build their nest
The little skylark, he sings all day
Then takes a well-earned rest
There are these fine green fields, on a beautiful day
Where little children come to play, and promise to meet next day
As evening cast her shadow and blackbird sings his song
He has only come to tell you, that night-time won't be long
And now the dawn comes creeping on, to make another day
We have the song of the thrush, to cheer us on our way
The rabbits they have their run around
And then they all go home by underground.

Thomas Grimwood

BELLS

Joyfully the bells will ring
The good news to foretell
To herald in the new-born *King*
The gift of *God's* own precious *Son.*

The angels sang the wonderful news;
The shepherds followed the star;
Led to the stable where the baby lay;
The kings came too from afar.

So rejoice and sing of this wonderful thing,
Tell the news abroad, shout it aloud,
That *Jesus* came into the world,
To be our glorious *Saviour.*

Let the bells ring out loud and clear
Telling all '*The King is here.*'
He came to bring *God's* peace on earth.
So we rejoice and sing of His worth
Of *Jesus* our blessed redeemer.

Sister Molly Billings SWJ

WHAT ARE YOU?

You're my breath
You're my eyes
You're my arms
You're my heart
You're my light
You're my dark
You're my moon
You're my stars
You're my winter
You're my summer
You're my autumn
You're my spring
To me you are my
    everything.

Jayne Rose Taylor

A LIFETIME

Some things only come with age
When you know you're turning your last page,
Of a life so precious you took for granted,
Now you look back at the things you've mantled,
The things you put off until tomorrow
While handling the happiness
The love and the sorrow.
Before you know it the years have flown,
You're getting old
Your kids are up and grown,
Where's time gone?
What's it all been for?
Is this our only life
Or is there more?
Thoughts remain inside of me
We only live once,
Or do we?

Joan Farlow

FREEDOM

Hold high the torch of freedom,
Light the world with the flame.
Hold high your head for the things you do
Your deeds in freedom's name.

Hold high the torch of freedom,
And keep it burning bright,
And may the flame keep spreading,
To set the world alight.

Hold high the torch of freedom
With all your might resist,
The tyrants and oppressors
Who use the iron fist.

And hold the torch of freedom high
Until the battle's won
For freedom is the birthright
Of every mother's son

Jim Quinn

SARAH

Small bundle in her mother's arms
She hardly showed her baby charms.
A few weeks passed and then you'd see
A dimpled cheek as she smiled at me
Before too long she crawled around
Making gurgling baby sounds.
When suddenly she'd start to talk.
By then she'd also learned to walk.
Then one day she would keep on chattering
As up the stairs you'd hear her clattering
She loved to give a kiss and hug
But in your heart you feel a tug
When her little face looked sad
When told off by her mom or dad.
All the family have to share her.
My little grand-daughter called Sarah.

M M Watts

A DAY RETURN PLEASE

The express train rushes down the track
Its noisy wheels going clickety-clack.
Speeding through fields both far and wide
With coaches swaying from side to side.

Rushing along at such a pace
You'd almost think it was in a race.
But being on time is its ultimate goal
As it chases through tunnels as black as coal.

The final bend comes into view
As evening mist follows morning dew.
People rise with a stretch and yawn
Like the early birds on a new day morn.

The driver slowly applies the brakes
For now isn't the time to make mistakes.
Passengers gather at doors closed tight
Soon to be opened when they all alight.

Into the dark they'll all disappear
Each to their homes both far and near.
The tired old train has given of its best
As throughout the day it has stood many tests.

People forget as they journey along
Just how many things could go wrong.
For although you've journeyed on a boat and a plane
There's nothing quite like a ride on a train.

Derek Kershaw

THE BULLY

This is the tale of Sammy Spry
Who thought he was a clever guy
On folk less fortunate than he
His pranks were practised constantly.
Watching his victims - pale with fright
Filled the bully with delight.

The local fellows tried like mad
To get the better of this cad.
Each time Sam Spry came out on top
And their brave efforts were a flop
Until a widow moved to town
And Sammy's world turned upside down.

She stood no more than five feet two
Her hair was red - her eyes were blue
And Sammy fell - as nature planned
Her every wish was his command
Then very soon up to the altar
She led him - like a lamb to slaughter.

No one was more amazed than he
Her tongue lashed at him constantly
But as the bully's life she wrecked
The more she gained his deep respect
All misdemeanours he did cease
And the village gained a welcome peace.

So if a bully you would be
Take this advice I offer free
Before you hurt some other guy
Recall the tale of Sammy Spry
A bully only spurns the weak
To camouflage *his* yellow streak!

Rose V Sutton

HIPS WIDE APART

Rehearsals are such an advantage, whatever the subject involved,
A stage presentation or concert, a speech or a joke to be told.
At the end of the war Norway's monarch, who'd been in UK
                                              for some years,
Was going back home to his subjects, our Navy escorting him there.

As the ship that was taking him over was to pass quite a large
                                              RN fleet.
The admiralty sent out an order, setting standards for each
                                              ship to meet.
The 'Birmingham' was such a vessel and the captain instructed
                                              his crew.
That for this auspicious occasion, a rehearsal would have to ensue.

All ratings not wanted for duties, like cooking, mess-cleaning,
                                              sick bay,
Were told to put on their best clothing, 'number ones' was the
                                              dress of the day.
At last came the time of rehearsal, on show a formidable force
Of well over five hundred ratings, inspected and shipshape of course.

Now the captain had told the commander to lead the three cheers
                                              for the King,
And Jimmy-the-One as we called him, expected perfection to bring.
So proudly he stood on a turret, a megaphone held in his hands.
And made it quite clear to the ship's crew, just how they'd obey
                                              his commands.

'Hip! . . . Hip!' Called out Jimmy, at a tempo so slow 'twas absurd,
But before the response could be shouted, the captain's voice
                                              everyone heard.
It came over the ship's broadcast system, words obviously right
                                              from the heart.
'Jimmy, that's not what is wanted, your hips are just too far apart!'

There followed a deafening silence, the commander being clearly upset.
While the five hundred crew suppressed laughter; a defaulter knew
what he would get!
For some seconds the silence continued, all present exploding within,
Then tension relieved by commander, whose features broke into a grin.

That signalled a volume of laughter unequalled in Royal Navy ships,
And the rest of the cheering rehearsal was light-hearted and loaded
with quips.
At the time of King Haakon's departure, the 'Birmingham'
cheered from the heart,
But the King didn't know we were cheering for
our 'Jimmy-with-hips-wide-apart'.

Norman Dallen

SQUASH

I saw two men playing squash today,
Oh what a game it is to play.
In little white shorts they were dressed,
Running around hardly stopping to rest.
Darting here, racing there,
Hitting the ball with little fear.
The way they scored was quite confusing,
Sometimes angry, sometimes amusing.
Racquets were swinging at an alarming pace,
The ball from wall to wall was placed.
'Drop-shot, good shot, volley ball' was cried,
I listened amazed, bewildered, wide-eyed.
The game was over, the winner beamed,
Off for a pint, on the bar they leaned.
I think I might try this game some day,
But 90 is a little too old to play!

D Hadfield

THE ELDERLY LADY OF SEATON

There is an old lady in Seaton, we see every day in the town,
She is so picturesque in her fashion, that visitors watch her spellbound;
Her clothes are of many bright colours, her hat is so cleverly made,
The trousers she wears sewn with patches, with colours red,
                                                yellow and jade.

The best part of our dear old lady is the way she will answer you back,
You tell her the day's warm and sunny, 'Silly sod' she will
                                                answer back:
We've seen her buy things in the shops here, and soon after
                                                give them away,
Standing in Windsor gardens to stop those people who pass by that day.

She must have been clever when younger, intelligent too I'm sure,
For her home-crocheted hat and trousers would take experts
                                                hours and more;
One day I shall miss the old lady, she's always a sight for sore eyes,
She'll sit on the bench near the pathway, eating her ham,
                                                cheese and pies.

A couple of lads in their teen years thought, 'here is a chance
                                                for some fun'
They taunted the old soul with cruel sneers, till her stick contacted
                                                their bums;
Now some days the weather is awful but don't think our lady
                                                stays home,
She'll sit on the bench in the rainfall, take a tot from her red socks,
                                                them roam.

I'm sure our old lady was pretty, I'm sure she was clever and good,
But now in her late years she's ready to answer lads well with
                                                her wood;
Now I can't tell you much about her, I feel she belongs where she is,
I'm sure I shall always look for her as long as our *old lady lives.*

W Herbert G Palfrey

DAUGHTER

'It's a girl Mr Thorpe,' Oh I felt such pride,
A joyous feeling deep inside,
Nature's beauty a joy to behold
Grey hair and stress as I grow old.

It all seemed great in the early years,
Life was fun and held no fears.
An impish smile, 'I luv oo Mum,
And no indication of problems to come.

We got through nappies and the first day at school,
Our daughter was happy as a general rule,
But then Mother Nature got her into a state,
With facial spots and a gain in weight.

Bitterness, anger, can't make any friends,
It seems that the anguish never ends.
We sent her to school miles away,
The decision would be different if we made it today.

Never gave her much money, always trying to save,
Perhaps she'll get more when we're both in our grave.
But now she's at college and if she uses her head
She'll set herself up for her life ahead.

Now we seem to be past all the main teenage ills,
But now my son is thirteen
Oh where are my pills?

Gary A Thorpe

TO SIR WITH LOVE

(Written for Mr Pickering's retirement from St Leonard's Junior School Hythe, after 30 years service)

He travelled all around the world
And ended up here teaching us.
If he could have foreseen what was coming,
He would have stayed on the Greyhound bus.

Here comes Sir for the final time to St Leonard's,
Last day before fulfilling all his dreams.
He's heading for the staff-room, quick,
Hide all the custard creams.

Mr Pickering, 'Sir' as we call you,
Thanks for all the great times that we've had,
Sharing lessons, jokes and sports days,
Your legs really aren't that bad.

The Spice Girls have got a sporty spice,
But not sporty compared to you.
Racquet in hand and plimsoles on,
Sir, can show them a thing or two.

Another line of little monsters,
Shuffles into his sun-filled room.
They'll all march out like Roman soldiers,
By the end of the afternoon.

You've taught mums and dads,
And their children
To do the best that they can,
What more could we ask of our teacher,
Mr Pickering what a nice man.

One last question before you leave Sir
Out through St Leonard's gates you pass,
Next time you teach in your short shorts,
Can I sit at the front of your class?

Jacky Page

MY DAD

You are someone I've always looked up to,
You always know what's right.
In fact I'll go so far as to say,
You've been my guiding light.

As a child, you'd sit me on your bike,
For hours we'd be gone.
And you always made sure we had holidays,
When most other kids had none.

You worked hard to get us some money,
The sacrifices that you made.
It couldn't have been easy,
The foundations that you laid.

You listen to my troubles,
Even though you have your own.
You taught me how to be strong,
'Don't let anyone put you down.'

Thank you Dad, for all you've done,
I appreciate it so much.
That's why I love you like I do,
No other man could ever touch.

Anita Flynn Brown

THIS SPECIAL DAY

This special day
When two hearts blend into one,
This special love,
As natural as rain and sun,
Two loves, a perfect match
Like white clouds on sky of blue,
Or, green grass, with flowers of golden hue.
This special day,
When family and friends look on with pride,
Sharon and Ian stand side by side
Waiting expectantly.
Him with a nervous smile,
She with a trembling lip maybe,
A glance, which says 'I love you'
A look in reply, 'I love you too.'
Then the words 'I promise, I do, I promise, I do'
The magic phrase 'man and wife.'
Holding them close for life,
Love's arms encircle,
Two lips meet
Keeping them safe in love's retreat.
So, the music starts,
As they walk hand in hand,
In their hearts will stay,
The memories, of this very special day.

K L Pusey

NAN

My nan used to live in the High Street
Her house was right by the Thames
We could see the ships from her windows
And we looked on the dockers as friends.
We loved to go and visit, she had such lovely things for tea
And she'd tell such wonderful stories, to my brother John and me.
She never used to nag us, or make us wipe our feet
She'd play with us and laugh with us and let us choose a sweet
From a big round tin, she kept on a shelf, 'Come on loves'
She'd say and let us help ourselves.
She had a smile for everyone, her face was never sad
And nobody would ever guess, the sorrow that she'd had.
A husband that had beaten her, loved children that had died.
Yet my nan bothered no one, she kept it all inside
Like a big dark secret, held out of sight
'I'm a widow' she would say. As if that put everything right.
My nan died during the war, a bomb fell in the dockside
And blew in her front door, there was dust and debris everywhere
Glass thick upon the ground and the plants that she
Used to love so much were scattered all around.
Dad just said 'Mother' then 'Mother' again
In a voice that was tight with emotion and pain
And my heart cried, because Nan had died
And I would never see her again.

My nan's house doesn't exist now, there's just an empty space
But when I walk the High Street, I see her smiling face.
She's standing at the window, waving her old sweet tin
And as I pass she calls to me 'Hey June gal come on in . . .'

June Pace

I AM THE LORD THAT HEALETH THEE -EXODUS 15:26
THE RIVER THAT BRINGS LIFE

I hear the River flowing, the River that brings life
Sustaining, gently lifting, flowing, through each part
The Spirit of the Living God reaching deep within my heart
Going back to the beginning of my life, given at conception,
As an innocent, helpless baby, I nestled in the womb,
But cruel words were spoken over me, cut through me like a knife,
Unseen hands came to harm me, tried to take my life.
Now unwanted and unloved, I wept within that womb.
Crying out for mercy to a cruel and murderous world.
Was there no one there to hear me, no one there to hear my cry?
No one there to hear the silent scream,
No one there to hear the anguished - Why?
Yes, someone did have mercy and did not allow me to die.
God looked down and saw me, placed His hands upon my life.
Now the Spirit of the Living God is flowing in-between,
Those parts hidden deep within me, those parts, until now unseen.
Healing all those broken pieces, damaged, ragged, torn,
Restoring and refreshing from the time that I was born.
He's led me to forgiveness of the hands that caused me harm,
He's poured Himself into those wounds, His *love* became my balm,
He's melted all the bitterness, taken anger, hurt and pain,
Now after all these years, I am free to live again.
He created me as His daughter, to be cherished, cared for and loved
This precious, wonderful gift of life, given by my Father from above.
I hear the River flowing I feel it deep within,
Soothing me, restoring, bringing comfort, making whole,
All those years of brokenness, the pieces now being restored.

Sandra Dean

THE CEASELESS WATCH

The little head rests heavy
hot and clammy too,
a mother's hand rests gently
the baby is but new.
The hours tick by with not a sign
the silent mother waits,
could this illness be benign?
The day it grows so late.
She prays in her mind, such heartfelt pleas,
She puts her faith in God
'Please don't take my baby Lord
I'll strive to be so good.'
She strokes the tender cheek and hand
her tears fall on the pillow,
day comes again, a bird is singing
upon the weeping willow.
A gasp, a breath and then relief
a bloom is on his cheek,
He opens up his dark brown eyes to hear his mother speak,
'My darling baby how I've longed to see you smile again
You'll play once more in splendid sun, and dance out in the rain.'
That night when all is quiet and still
the mother sits once more,
beside her peaceful, sleeping son
but this time she is sure
her prayers were answered, now she must
be sure to do her best,
She promises and then she takes, some happy, blessed rest.

Cheryl Mann

HEART TO HEART

A Message For Mum

I sit in my house,
and stare into space,
hoping and praying,
there was another place,
for me to go,
and calm myself down,
to try and not let my mother know,
that all I really can do is frown,
I have hopes and dreams,
that might just come true,
and if they happen,
I'll still always love you.

Mother's Reply

I know about your hopes and dreams,
I see them in your eyes,
I know how much you want to go,
it comes as no surprise,
but you're still young,
with time to grow,
don't wish your life away,
for when you step into the world,
and start to live your way,
you'll realise how hard it is,
and will suffer stress and fear,
so enjoy this safety while you can,
it's only one more year.

Dawn & Corinne Tuck (15)

BELLA

A puppy in my life again,
What joy awaits us all!
But like all babes, training's a must
And that on me will fall.

To choose a name is difficult,
There is a lengthy list;
Cherry, Lady, Lucky, Bella,
Which one can't I resist?

Must be patient, but very soon
This pup will come to stay,
With love and kisses and great fun,
I know she'll make my day.

She's made my day, I'll not deny,
Our black bundle of fun;
With head held high and tail all cocked,
She's mischief on the run.

Socks and shoes and towels too,
She steals with such delight,
Frustration grows, but anger fades,
She's such a jolly sight.

Our Bella really is the 'tops',
And growing more each day.
Unless sleeping, playing, walking,
She loves to have her say.

Now one year on, we've settled down,
And days ahead unfurl;
Long walks on coast path or on beach,
We will enjoy our 'girl'.

Janet Bowen

JOURNEY OF A LIFETIME

In the autumn of my years, I rest and close my eyes,
My body may be feeble now, but my mind is still alive.
I remember as if 'twere yesterday, a young boy running free,
Climbing trees, exploring caves, rushing home for tea.
Potato pie and home-made bread, the smells that filled my head,
Bread and dripping by the fire, a bowl of stew instead.
Then time passed by I stretched my wings, I learnt to feel my way,
Through the good times and the bad times, through the work and
through the play.
I remember towns I visited, places where I'd been,
People I once knew and loved, sights that I have seen.
Even bad times I recall, times of pain and woe,
Things you shouldn't have to do, places you shouldn't go.
Times that I've been hungry, no hope, no work, no bed.
Things I've done just to survive, things that's best not said,
But better times prevailed, bad times turned to good.
I built a rich and happy life, the best one that I could,
Fond memories in my head abound, I still touch every one.
They'll keep me going, young at heart, till my last breath has gone.
I'll ne'er forget this life of mine, the stories I could tell,
The sights, the sounds, the tastes, the smells, as I sit here and dwell.

Jeff Nixon

WHO MADE THESE?

See the sunshine,
See the rain,
See the hailstone,
See the gale,
See the flowers,
See the trees,
Do you wonder
Who made these?

See the birds, they fly so high
Soaring high into the sky,
See the clouds so soft and white,
Feel the sun so warm and bright,
Do you wonder?
Can you tell?
He who made them made them well.

Sylvia Cole

EVERY POEM TELLS A STORY

Many, many years ago my small son said to me
'I'll never, ever leave you Mum - married to *you* I'll be!'
And as I laughed and held him close, I gently tried to say
'One day, my love, you'll meet a girl and want to go away.'
Those childhood days sped by so fast, I felt so very blest,
My daughter and two sons I had, of life, the very best,
And then that day - of course it came, the wedding bells were rung
Their vows were made, their prayers were said
And favourite hymns were sung.
A new life had begun for them, and so it had for me!
That empty room a symbol of a sort of misery -
A backward step I had to take, the longest of my life,
A mother-in-law I had become, my son now had a wife.
I vowed I'd do my best for them, but would I be allowed?
This girl already had a mum, I knew she'd do them proud.
And yet this daughter-in-law of mine was wise beyond her years,
The babies came, she let *me* share, there was no need for tears.
My daughter-in-law how cold it sounds,
I quickly hasten to add,
Our daughter-in-love - she has become to me and to his dad.

Valerie Baker

THE CHRISTMAS PRAYER

'Isn't she beautiful' Sarah thought, as she gazed in the window
of the store.
The doll stood erect, her blue eyes unblinking. But just for a moment
it looked like she was winking. Sarah knew as she stood there,
her face pressed close to the pane, that the Christmas they'd all enjoyed
last year wasn't going to happen again.
'For times are hard, and gifts will be few,' her mother had said.
'for Tom and for you. I'm sorry love but it has to be. With your dad
unemployed, there's no money you see!'

That night Sarah said her prayer. 'Dear Lord Jesus, I know
You're there. Please can You find my dad some work, something he
can do real good? I will go to Sunday School Lord Jesus if You would.
Soon it will be Christmas, Your own special day. Please give us Your
blessing, and hear me when I pray.'

The night before Christmas they put up the tree (young Tommy was
crawling around). Decorations were hung, fairy lights danced, suddenly
there came a new sound. 'Listen Mum, it's Dad and he's singing,'
Sarah said as she jumped to her feet. Sure enough the words of the carol
'Good King Wenceslas' rang down the street. 'Look what I've got for
my two favourite girls. And for my wonderful boy,' said Dad as he
came through the door with a rush, dropping parcels his face full of joy.
'Whatever has happened,' his wife asked. 'Where did you get all
of this?' 'Don't worry sweetheart,' her husband laughed, as he gave
her a hug and a kiss. 'You know that job I did for Harry nearly six
months ago? Well, he's come good and he paid me. He's doing well
now and so, he wants me to be his new partner. I can start after
Christmas, my love. My carpentry work pleased him greatly. It's just
like a gift from above.'

Well! Sarah stared in amazement. She could hardly believe what
she'd heard. 'But I . . . I said a prayer for you Daddy,' she said.
'and Jesus *did* hear every word.'

'Of course He did poppet, He's like that.' Her father lifted her onto his knee. 'And I've got something to give you. We can put it on top of the tree.'

And out of his bag, came the doll with blue eyes, that Sarah had loved at first sight. 'Oh thank you Jesus!' she whispered, as she knelt by her bedside that night.

June M Jobborn

PASSING DAYS

    Blow soft wind
blow the sorrow from my heart,
    sing sweet dancing leaves
sing a song before we pass and part.

    How shall we leave this peace?
Bright waters gleaming in the bay,
    little rocking boats turning their heads
so bravely into the waves of yesterday.

    How this gracious, gallant house
gleams white, then brighter in the sun,
    her windows watch so patiently
each waiting day, seems scarce begun.

    A hand has loved this place.
Still keeps the lawns deep carpeting,
    no highest hedge, no fragrant flower
still holds, our own swift harvesting.

    Clouds now cross the blue of day,
shadows trail across the green of grass,
    shelter us, when soon we leave,
and let us sigh, and gently pass.

Jean Mary Orr

TORN APART

Even though you're far away
I think about you every day
I see your smile, your gorgeous face
Your tender kiss, your warm embrace.

You're far away, but not by choice
I hear a whisper, I hear your voice
It seems to tell me 'Don't be blue'
And tells me that you love me too.

I miss you more each passing day
I love you totally in every way
I sometimes feel that you are here
And the miles between us disappear.

I think of all the times we've shared
No other love on earth compared
For you are the one I dream about
My heart is breaking without a doubt.

I long for the day you are by my side
All my feelings I will not hide
We'll make love the whole night through
I'll show you how much I really love you.

So until the day I'm by your side
My love for you I cannot hide
I lay awake most every night
My falling tears I cannot fight.

I hope you feel as much for me
As I do for you as you can see
I love you sweetheart with all my heart
And hate us being so far apart.

We've said goodbye, but not for long
For in your arms, I know I belong
I've loved you from the very start
Now that you're gone, I'm torn apart.

Joanne Davison

LIFE IN THE FAST LANE

I'm driving down the motorway,
Speeding at seventy-five,
My banger's purring along the road,
I'm glad to be alive!

I'm reaching the exit
I'm going to take
My hand on the gears,
My foot on the brake.

I'm nearing my village,
I'm homeward bound,
And that's when I hear it,
Oh God, what's that sound?

Rattle, rattle, knock, knock, grind,
Well now I'm in a fix,
I think I'll pull onto the next parking spot,
And give it a good few kicks.

But the temperature's rising, into the red,
Now the water will certainly boil,
'Cos I couldn't afford a service,
And I forgot to check the oil!

Denise Jones

OUR STORY

I met you when I was at school,
At first I thought we'd keep it cool.
But as the time went slowly by,
The feelings got deeper, between you and I.

It wasn't much longer, when we really knew
That our love was blooming, together we grew.
We knew that we wanted, both you and me,
A lifetime together seemed heavenly.

The wedding was special, when I look back now,
To the day when we promised each other our vow.
Twenty years old and happy to be
The wife of my husband, for all to see.

Good times, tough times, we had them all,
Our love never faltered, or took a fall.
We had some news, we were so glad,
To both become a mum and dad.

I gave birth to a baby boy,
Your face was full of pride and joy.
We couldn't see what lay ahead,
All the nights up out of bed.

But we got through it, you and I,
For a marriage to work, you both have to try.
Give and take and plenty of care,
Lots of love, be willing to share.

Now we've been married for nineteen years,
You've been there through my hopes and fears.
I thank you darling, for all you do,
That's why I always will love you.

Caroline L Lillystone

THE PLUCKSGUTTER GAZETTE

Our flourishing little weekly, the
'Gazette' for which you wait,
Hereby reports the great success
Of marrow over watercress,
In this year's village fete.

We held it just a week ago
Upon the village green,
With competition very high
For choicest fruit or nicest pie
That the judge had ever seen.

To Mrs Chipps, the vicar's wife,
The dreadful task did go
Of judging who should have the prize
For vegetables, and there were cries
Of joy, when she chose Joe.

For Joe had grown a marrow that
Was fit for any queen.
He'd watered it and cared for it
And now upon it he could sit,
It was so large and green.

Poor Mrs Chipps could not decide
At first just what to do;
For Albert's crop of watercress,
She said she really must confess,
Was too good to be true.

However, first prize went to Joe,
And here's a treat for *you*;
For on this page, next week, you'll read
About the planting of the seed
From which the marrow grew.

Jennifer Munro

MY WIFE

I know someone who is trusting, kind and true
Who always lifts your spirits when you are feeling blue
Is always ready to intercede if opinions don't work out
A person always true to their word and there isn't any doubt
Someone who never moans or cries but just gets on with life
It's just great to know this person and to have her as a wife.

She is the person who always gives her time to every point of view
Makes the ultimate sacrifices and always follows them through
Gives of her best even when stressed and leads by example every time
Has qualities in every field and never goes into anything blind
Is discerning, co-operative and a good judge in all aspects of life
And it's good to know she is around and to have her as a wife

A person who can be determined in all important matters of living
Making sure each one plays an active role in both the receiving
                                      and the giving
Not watering down for the sake of it but being a pillar firm
In control as far as possible, dealing with each problem in turn
And showing always that warmth and affection through any
                                      bitterness and strife
She sure can read between the lines and radiates confidence
                                      that's a wife

And as a mother and a wife and the many other jobs it takes
She sets a busy schedule with the many demands all this makes
From early in the morning till the sun goes down at night
Clothes have to be washed, meals provided and that ironing,
                                      oh what a delight
All this and much more is taken for free as we carry on through life
Never thinking sometimes of the workload involved and lending
                                      a hand to a wife

Yes that person sometimes taken for granted and not recognised as such
The fulcrum of the family who everyone depends on so much
And when the day's work is over for most her work continues to run
Still giving that caring commitment on which all of us rely upon
And even when things outside get tough and maybe
                                        rumours become rife
It's great to have someone to talk to, that ever-listening ear of a wife

A person dedicated to all the family needs and the traditional
                                        family spirit
Believing what's ours is one thing but we must always be
                                        ready to share it
And give guidance and wisdom to everyone to ensure life's
                                        important things are known
Usually the person who books the holiday and tells us
                                        where we're going
And when there are troubled times in our lives and our reactions
                                        are as sharp as a knife
She leads us away stating tomorrow's another day what a blessing
                                        it is to have such a wife

A J McCourt

LIFE'S JOURNEY

I have seen the miracles
    I have heard the voice
I have felt the awesome power
    And I have made the choice.
I have climbed the mountain top
    I have crossed the mighty sea
I have crawled the barren desert
    And came face to face, with me.

Alison Forbes

ODE TO BUSHMILLS

Crystal waters flow down to the sea
Along the bush where the salmon run free
From the basalt rock of the Antrim coast
Come raise a glass with me and toast
To the world's oldest whiskey that yet distils
In a quaint wee town they call Bushmills
With a hint of sherry, vanilla and honey
Sure no better a dram you could buy for your money
It all began back in sixteen-o-eight
And the age-old process is still used of late
With its triple distilled to be smooth and pure
On a cold winter's night, a hot bush is the cure
So come again, and fill up my glass
And let us praise a pure touch of class

Nevin Mccloy

MY LIFE

When I was one I learnt to talk and fight
At two I could play the piano with all my might
Then at three I could write and draw a face
At four I could read and do ballet dressed in lace
Next came five and I learnt to do my shoes and swim
Come six I climbed trees and rode bikes with Jim
At seven I tied laces and wrote joined-up
Poetry and trampolining at eight - bouncing up
At nine I petted at the hamster that was mine
And now I'm older because I'm ten
I've started French so I'll learn to write again!

H Montgomery

ENCOUNTER

Once, long ago, I met a gnome
When I was lost, in deep despair
He led me to the pathway home
And gave me tender loving care.

He let me cry, he held me near
I felt protected, safe, secure.
He understood the pain and fear
And what I still had to endure.

He somehow let me lean on him
And draw upon his strength and love
Until the pain and hurt within
Had eased and I could look above

The wilderness of paths untrod
To see ahead a source of light.
I fearfully began to plod
Towards this, knowing it was right.

He radiated warmth and joy
And taught me how to love, to be.
He showed me how to change my life
That I might learn to run, be free.

Time has passed, I'm stronger now
Learning how to trust and feel
Yet ever will I know his love
His courage and his care so real.

His sensitivity touched my soul
Entered my centre, my inner core.
No matter where I travel now,
My love is. Forever more.

Jennifer Densham

WILLIAM

There once lived a man called William, he had daughters
    three and a wife,
He worked many years as a miller, well practically all of his life.
He was the life and soul of the party, and sang at the drop of a hat,
He could dance and play ukulele, his whole repartee off pat.
This man was a kind loving father, to his daughters three,
He was always there to turn, he would listen, and give sympathy.
Then there were his brothers and sisters, he gave them his love
    and his care,
Their parents died young and left them, but William, the eldest,
    was there.
He worked and took care of the family, they repaid with
    devotion for life,
And it was, at this point in time, he took Martha, a neighbourhood
    girl for his wife.
The years passed and William grew older, then they retired him
    from the mill,
It was all that he'd known for his lifetime, and about this time he fell ill.
Then Martha took care of William, they moved house and a new
    life began,
For with this house came a garden, and William became a new man,
He tended this, his first garden, with all of his love and his care,
And soon the loveliest flowers, and beautiful roses grew there.
And one summer's day when the roses bloomed bright,
He said, 'When I'm no longer here, the roses will be,' and he was right.
Then William learned he had cancer, the family were so desolated,
That they responded, with loving support, cannot be understated.
But as he faced the last battle, he'd greet you with his gentle smile,
He'd be resting in bed, just waiting, for us to stay for a while.
Then early one April morning, he left us so quietly then,
We were there, by his bed when his life went, we'll never see
    his like again.

The church was full of people, who had come to say goodbye, to Bill,
To them he was husband and father, brother and friend, but still,
As the minister started the service, he repeated, 'This man, this man,'
    and I felt sad,
I wanted to stand and state loudly, this man's name was William,
    he was our beloved Dad.

Eileen Cuddy Buckley

EVERY POEM

As I sit alone I wonder, of a lifetime that's passed by
Things I do, the stress, the worry, I can find no reason why
Then I think of days gone by, of my life and family
It gives me hope as I remember, all the love there used to be
Brothers, sisters close together, complete with loving Mam and Dad
All the fun, and yes some quarrels, the best times we ever had
Each day for us was, 'quite a struggle' times they were so hard you see
A next-door neighbour, we called Auntie, such a special friend was she
Often taking us on outings, to ease the load from Mam and Dad
Christmas time for us so special, presents from Auntie, we all had
A married woman now am I, with six children of my own
Yes I've neighbours, none so special, like the neighbour
we have known
This special Auntie's name is Mair, played a big part in our life
When both our mam and dad departed, the pain it cut just like a knife
Mair was there to help and comfort, up until the very end
To us just not a next-door neighbour, but a close and special friend
Life's friendship carries on forever, one true friend Mair's always there
Mam and Dad would be proud of you, for giving us children
such love and much care.

Katrina Minney

JENNIFER REES

Jennifer Rees of 3A
Are you still alive today?
And did you consider it a curse
To read this book of children's verse?
As you scanned the relevant page
Did your eyes go out of focus
At so much fanciful hocus-pocus,
Or were you enticed from an early age
By Wordsworth, Keats and Coleridge?
Was alliteration a pointless chore,
And metaphor a dreaded bore.
Or do you carry in your head
The pertinent things that poets have said?
Jennifer Rees of 3A
(Though you must be almost dead)
Do you while the time away
Rhyming couplets in your bed?

Olwen Smyth

TWO FAT LADIES

Two fat ladies sitting side by side
Two fat ladies trying to decide
Should we get fatter or
Should we try to slim
What a decision
Where does one begin
Two fat ladies feeling rather glum
Looked at each other
Decision time had come
One said to the other feeling full of fun
Let's wait until tomorrow
I think we'll have a bun

Denise Emms

UNREQUITED LOVE

He's there again, that handsome man
There must be some way that I can
Catch his eye and make him see
There's no-one in this world but me.
I've seen him many times before
Standing just inside the door
If only he would look my way
I'd smile, but not a word I'd say.
It's not considered very nice
For polite young girls to break the ice.
To flirt in church is not allowed,
Unlikely too, with one's head bowed.
Through anthem, hymn and sermon long
My heart ascends on wings of song.
The service over, now's my chance,
My thoughts engaged in merry dance
I drop my hymn book at his feet
Those shiny shoes, so black, so neat.
He moves, excited shivers bind me,
He's gone to speak to the girl behind me . . .
I'll never, ever, love another,
Not my neighbour, nor my brother.
The Good Book tells me this I should do,
But it might have told the young man too . . .

Carol Wright

GOD'S PRECIOUS GIFT

God gave me a very precious gift,
He gave me a little son,
His hair is fair and his eyes are very blue
He has a very fair complexion
And he's tiny too.

Each night I put him in his cot
And then he started to cry
I told him I loved him very much,
Then I sang him a lullaby.
Years have rolled by since that special day.

Now he is a grown-up son
And he's very caring too,
I love him very much,
Now he looks after me,
Because I'm his mum.

Elma Evelyn Kirkham

DUBLIN MOUNTAINS

The Dublin Mountains are a sight to be seen,
With all the different shades of green.
Take a walk up there,
You'll feel great, from the fresh, clean air.

But beware!
As when night falls
You may hear whispering calls,
From the little fellows called leprechauns.
They are small and wear green,
And don't like to be seen.
Catch one if you can

And from this little man,
You'll receive three wishes,
However, take a fourth and he'll turn vicious.

So remember, being greedy is not the key,
But content and happy is how you should be!

Sinéad Carter

THE LITTLE DOG'S PRAYER

Alone, dejected, the little dog sat,
No comfy chair, no nice warm mat,
Just cold night air and traffic around;
He could hardly bear to hear the sound.

His limbs just twitched with fear and fright.
He would never make it through the night.
Though the screech of brakes often rent the air,
There was nothing he could do but just sit there.

Would the car come back with the people he had known,
Or would he stay here to die all alone?
In a state of shock, he couldn't move,
He just prayed for help and the warmth of love.

Then in the damp and dark came a blinding light
And the hand of help in that dark chill night.
He was lifted close by a strong warm arm
And taken away from that place of harm.

He was lying soon in a cosy room,
Where he couldn't hear the traffic's boom.
Warm, well-fed and lavished with care;
Someone must have heard that little dog's prayer.

T B Chadwick

LIFE

What is life? some people say,
to some it's just another day.
They moan about summer, winter,
autumn and spring.
They are life's moaners,
with them you can't win.
Life is what you make it,
we all do have a choice.
We can delight in so many things,
like when birds sing out in full voice.
Butterflies flittering on flowers,
the hum of busy bees,
the wonderful beauty of a sunset
with its many shades of red.
The beautiful smile of a baby
as you tuck it down in its bed.
Life has so many joys to give,
so never moan and complain about life,
enjoy it; live and let live.

Patricia Gray

DEAFNESS

There's a silent world around us,
In which you and I reside,
We cannot hear the people singing,
Or the travelling cars outside.

We cannot hear the birds that sing,
That herald each new day,
And all those modern pop groups
Are just silent worlds away.

We cannot hear a baby's cry
Instinct tells us something's wrong.
The canary singing in its cage,
Is for us a muted song.

But there's beauty all around us
Which we witness with our eyes,
And though our world's a silent one
The world we see's a big surprise.

Gordon Barnett

THE CHOCOLATE DISASTER

Little children like a tasty treat, and chocolate is the thing to eat.
A bar of chocolate is just fine, but somewhere you must draw the line.
This creamy tasty melting goo, is great for kids and grown-ups too.
Jane's parents didn't know, that chocolate ends in tears and woe
So they let their darling child, go tasty chocolate-eating wild.
One bar a day, then two and three, a bar before dinner, a bar after tea.
Jane started putting on weight, but still she ate and ate and *ate!*
All her money she would save, to satisfy her chocolate crave.
Jane's parents begged her to stop, but not until she'd reached the top.
Jane yelled, 'No, I shall not have a rest, the caramel bars are the best.'
Jane's tum got that big until no more, could she fit through the door.
This chocolate problem got really bad, it drove everyone
completely mad.

Then one hot summer's morning, Jane's parents woke up yawning.
When from their darling daughter's room, they heard a loud
mighty *boom!*
They went into Jane's room and feared the worst,
Found that their precious Jane had *burst!*
All her pieces were on the floor, heart, lungs and chocolate galore.
Let that be a lesson to you, or you'll end up like Jane too!

Sarah Williams (12)

THE BLACKSMITH AND THE FARMER'S DAUGHTER

She had sun-kissed cheeks and kindly brown eyes.
She loved the young blacksmith but she was wise;
She waited calmly for him to court her,
'Perhaps today!' mused the farmer's daughter.

Her Pa called her 'Jim' for before her birth
He had prayed hard for a son to till the earth.
He taught her well how to plough, sow and reap,
How to milk his cows and to tend his sheep.

One wash-day her Ma called her. With a sigh,
Unwilling, she hung the clothes out to dry.
The shy blacksmith came just then and it seems
He sees her at last, the girl of his dreams.

Arms up-stretched, windblown, her long dark hair flows.
What youth and beauty! In panic he knows
He must not waste anymore time, no delay.
He must tell her of his love now, today.

Banns were called. Wedding bells rang. They were one.
Their love was blessed with the birth of their son.
She nursed her babe and cared for their small house,
Fulfilled and content with her blacksmith spouse.

'Missus!' The young lad hammered on the door.
'The gaffer's hurt bad!' He lay on the floor,
Kicked by a nervous horse. Cradling his head,
She soothed him, denying that he was dead.

Try as she might, her home she could not keep,
When they were leaving she tried not to weep.
Carrying the boy, her father brought her
Back to her mother, his grieving daughter.

In her memory their love lay frozen in time,
Beautiful, unspoiled and untouched by age, sublime.

Mary Birch

I'M SORRY

I was so sure
Of all that I knew
I didn't see
What I was doing to you

I closed my eyes
When I should have stopped to see
That you and I
Were living unhappily

I didn't hear you
Too deep my head in the sand
I should have realised
Loneliness can be where I stand

I should have questioned
When the crack began to appear
I guess I was
Just too afraid, what I feared

I'm sorry, I'm sorry
I love you
I'm sorry, I'm sorry
You love me too.

J C Walters

MUCK MAGNETS!

Snotty noses and knotted hair,
Grubby shirts we just don't care!

Mud-caked shoes and grass-stained socks,
Torn and patched trousers, creased and crumpled frocks!

Chocolate covered mouths and dirt-streaked cheeks,
Cracked and scratched glasses, trousers with no seats!

Oil plastered hands and grazed knobbly knees,
From fiddling with bike and climbing conker trees!

From fiddling with bike chains
And climbing conker trees

Muck magnets they may be and cheeky monkeys too!
But their mums all love 'em despite what they do!

Tara Dougal (12)

THE SEASONS OF MY LIFE

Spring is the beginning of everything new
Spring was the time when I found you
As the birds began to sing and the flowers to grow
You came into my life and I began to know
The warmth of each day and the joy of each night
As the sun caressed the earth you held me tight

The spring turned to summer and the earth was ablaze
We loved thro' the nights and laughed thro' the days
We walked down the street with the wind in our hair
Like the beasts of the fields we hadn't a care
Like nature around us how could we not know
With all of these things our love had to grow

Then summer turned to autumn and the leaves turned to gold
I began to shiver was your love turning cold?
Like a tiny flower reaching up to the sky
Without my sun I would curl up and die
Spring was gone, summer, autumn too
I began to feel I was losing you

With the passing of autumn the winter came
Bringing the cold, the frost, and the rain
The earth was covered with a blanket of snow
And so my love I began to know
Like the flowers we'll sleep until the spring
Then reawaken and begin again

Joan Hartland

ENDOMETRIOSIS

'Endometriosis' is what the doctor said
As I lay waiting on my hospital bed.
'What on earth is that?' I asked
Wondering if my fear was well masked.
'Bits of your endometrium have gone elsewhere'
The whys and wherefores she didn't seem to care.
'You've a follow-up check-up in six weeks' time,
You're to see a Specialist, that will ease your mind.'
A small consolation, they've found something at last,
'It's all in your mind' I was told in the past.
Repeating my symptoms over and over,
My womb beginning to feel like a bag from a hoover!
I know that I've got to put up with this pain,
Believe me, it's better than thinking I was going insane!

Ann Elizabeth Hurley

VILLAGE KIDS

Village kids, their mother's pearls
Live inside another world.
Creepy woods for scary haunting,
Old stick guns for woodland hunting,
Broomstick horses gallop neighing,
Hollow oaks, good for hiding.

Making gangs with secret places,
Wary of inquiring faces.
By the pond with stocking nets
Stickleback fish and tiny froglets,
Whirley-bugs and water skeeters,
Jam jars full of unknown creatures.

Girls collecting wild posies,
Boys neglecting snotty noses.
Packed-up lunch for paper chases,
Tripping over undone laces.
Peeling the bag off sticky sweets,
Pocket-matured for weeks and weeks.

Chair leg bat, tree stump wickets
Tip and run when playing cricket.
Red sun sets to echoed shouts
In warm dry air the batsman's out.
Daytime ends, bedtime's nearing,
A parent's call . . . ears not hearing.

Up the stairs, wash in seconds,
Read in bed until sleep beckons.
Tired bodies with angel faces
Drifting off to distant places.
More things to do, games for playing,
Wars to win and dragon slaying.

Village kids, their mother's pearls,
Live inside another world.

Malcolm Hockham

BROKEN SPIRIT . . .

Broken spirit, bent in two,
Just what will become of you?
What of all your hopes and dreams?
What of all your well-planned schemes?
Where's your confidence and pride?
Now you only wish to hide.
Hide that unexpected shame.
Hide the hurt and all that pain.
Where's the bliss you once pretended?
Upside down, your life's suspended.

Face the truth, the damage done.
Peel the layers, one by one.

Hush, now listen, what's that sound?
Silence that will turn you 'round.
Gently, weaknesses revealed.
Silently, your spirit's healed.

Stella Margaret Dyer

SPARE JUST A MOMENT

When you speak and look at me
Do not act upon my disability
See me the person
Who I am
Spare just one moment

We are here and here to stay
No use turning the other way
Spare just one moment
Tomorrow it could be you
A car crash, riding accident out of the blue
Illness, attack
No turning back
I pray it never happens to you

Spare just one moment
Before you say
Sorry we have no vacancies today
We may be just who you are looking for
So please think twice
Before you show us the door.

We are happy, willing workers
Just give us the chance to show
Our talents to you
Our training, our patience
Our dedication will then shine through
Spare just one moment
One day it could be you.

Thank you for giving me the job
To work daily as most people do
Thank you for giving me the time
For a relaxed and caring interview.

We are disabled, but still our brains
Need stimulation and association
With workmates to share

Thank you for all who assist us every day
With love and care
To help us on our way
Thank you for those moments.
Many of us can manage on our own
And like to retain independence
In our own homes
Many cannot manage
And need the help of others
To see us on our way
Thank you for those moments.

To all employers
            If each company employed one of us
            Then none of us
            Would be out of work.

            So we thank you
            For sparing us
            Just a moment.

Stella Hughes

THE ROAD-SIDE SHRINE

The cross stood high above the lonely hill,
The flowers were fresh; the memories fresher still:
'Twas on a winter's night in recent time
The road had claimed its victim - number nine.
There was no need for this last sacrifice
For on the road were warning signs marked *'Ice'*.
The summer came and sunshine filled the glen,
But winter follows - awaiting number ten.
Man thinks his wits against the elements suffice,
But has no answer to the killer known as *'Ice'*.

William J Bartram

A POCKET FULL OF TREASURE

My son's pocket full of treasures,
tell their tale of seasonal pleasures,
of eggshell pieces found in spring
amongst a mass of tangled string.

In summer its pebbles, shells and grains of sand
never escaping a little boy's hand.
There's lolly sticks, wrappers too,
a catapult, and my lost tube of glue!

As autumn arrives the conker reigns,
with acorns, blackberries and other remains.
All precious, all wanted and missed if mislaid
all tucked into pockets with seams all frayed.

Then winter brings berries and pine cones,
and other treasures he's found,
some delightful - and some not,
all things he's found on the ground.

And tucked deep in the pocket occasionally,
a crumpled little note - only for me.
A note to a mother from her six-year-old son,
just four words, scribbled quickly . . .
          I love you, Mum.

Deborah Sheppard

THE DENTIST

Sitting in the waiting room waiting to be seen,
In comes the dentist like a long thin bean
And says, 'Next, please,'
But first he has a sneeze.

I knew he'd say next, 'Take a seat.'
Suddenly I heard a sudden beat
Coming from the door,
I knew he'd get the pliers out, but first I heard a snore . . .

. . . and the light he lit.
The dentist said, 'Jump up, it won't hurt a bit.'
But I knew it would 'cause I'd been before -
Just by talking about it my mouth became so sore.

'Please get on the chair now,' said the dentist,
'You're third on the dental list,'
He got out a piece of string,
And went *ping* . . .

. . . and he even tied it to my tooth.
I wanted an ambulance and where was the nearest booth?
Mummy said, 'Keep calm,'
But I couldn't 'cause he was doing too much harm.

The pain got worse and worse
So I wanted a nurse.
He slammed the door
And my tooth fell to the floor.

Blood streamed down to my face,
I wanted to race,
I clambered out of the seat
And started to my feet.

Jessica Flood

IN MEMORY OF VID

We met in June nineteen forty-four
And on the day and upon the hour
There was born a friendship firm and true
That wavered not but forever grew.
For thirty-five years Vid was my friend,
The blessing was mine - but blessings end.
Vid came in, in eighteen ninety-three,
By two decades he preceded me.
At seventy inch we were one height
But I lost out by a stone in weight.
As landed neighbours most days we met
And talked - not just on the farming set!
Always either had a tale to tell
And Vid's sense of fun matched mine so well.
We laughed at this life an awful lot,
At the theatre's comedy spot.
At football when excitement had gone
For if it was there we found the fun.
At rugger and golf, Vid had his fling -
Boxed with skill in the amateur ring.
He was my mentor when we did touch
On Gladstone, Lloyd George, Baldwin or such.
Four years Vid fought in the Kaiser's war
And resented not its lasting scar.
He often talked of the comradeship
That lightened the load of trench hardship.
On Christmas Eve, as year followed year,
We met in church, we were always there,
Enjoying the carols and the choir.
He loved to sing and I did admire
The rich deep voice which he never lost,
I think that is when I miss Vid most.

Sandy Murdoch

WELCOME HOME

The heavy front door gave a long loud creak as it swung open wide,
I thought I heard a voice say 'Come in' as I stepped warily inside.
The aroma of a bygone era enveloped me as I crept
toward the empty bedroom where once, others had slept.

There I saw a big brass bed with lace embroidered sheets,
the glow of a lamp the smell of lavender, strewn about my feet.
I tiptoed into the sitting room, afraid to disturb this 'peace',
catching a glimpse of old photographs, of lives that now have ceased.

A log fire crackled in the cold dusty grate, its flames dancing
along the walls,
a grandfather clock ticked in the ghostly silence outside in
the empty hall.
I turned around as I heard the sound of a trolley being set for tea,
with crocheted cloths and china cups as if it were meant for me!

My footsteps echoed around the silent room as I walked out through
the old French doors
into the garden, decaying now but once it was loved, I'm sure.
The derelict buildings stood silently amid the tangled
branches and weeds,
a kind of peace, like filigree lace, hung on the old apple trees.

Someone whispered 'Welcome home' it barely reached my ears,
or was it just the gentle breeze playing with my hair?
I turned and looked toward the house, standing empty and alone,
I smiled and it smiled back at me, I knew then that I had come home . . .

Dany Sherlock

THE PARK

The park is the place I love to be
With my family and friends, all there with me
I love the different rides, so big and bright
To see the children on them, squealing and laughing with delight

The swing goes higher when Mummy gives a push
Higher and higher, my tummy tingles, the wind blows awhoosh
And just then I think I can't stand any more
Mummy stops pushing, the swing slowly stops, my feet touch the floor

The merry-go-round in bright yellow, red and green
It's the fastest and best merry-go-round I've ever seen
It starts off real slow, the speed gradually gets faster
Our mummy's and daddy's face goes blurred, as we spin around past

The see-saw is scary when you come down with a bump
But it's also very funny when your friend goes down with a thump
Our tummies turn over and we giggle and laugh
When up in the air we can see the ice cream van, down the path

The slide is my favourite, it's very big and high
It's got many steps, that nearly reach up to the sky
When I get to the top of them, I wobble a bit and sit
Then down I come, down I come, off I come, soft bark on the floor I hit

It's been another good day, I've enjoyed every minute
Our sweety papers and packets, Mummy told us to bin it
We all feel tired but happy, just like in a dream
'Come on,' Mummy says, ' let's finish off the day
            With a really big ice cream.'

Wendy Pearce

FALTERING STEPPES

Russia now, is in the red,
The rouble is completely dead,
To the whole world, owes a debt
Which they will not forget.

People queue for hours at banks for money,
When cash runs out, will not be funny,
There is no leader, or any law,
Soon could be a civil war.

Again, there could be an iron curtain,
To guide the people, this is certain,
This time, will not get out of hand,
A powerful leader, they will understand.

Slave labour, on all State farms,
Soldiers, will again take up arms,
Secrecy and suspicion everywhere,
A show of strength, in Red Square.

Once more there could be a Soviet bloc,
Made up from many Oriental stock,
A world power, for a long time sleeping,
Its tentacles reaching outwards, creeping.

Robert Thompson

OH WHY?

Oh why did we go and get them?
Why did Rhett and Scarlet come to stay.
They've created messes and mayhem,
each and every night and day.

Our families when they visit,
say 'Oh aren't their faces sweet.'
Then I show all our treasured things,
that they have tried to eat.

They jump upon the furniture,
pull my washing off the line.
Then sit upon their hind legs,
when we sit down to dine.

My pretty flowered garden,
it's now looking rather sad.
They've bitten off the flower heads,
it really is *too* bad.

You may ask, why have we kept them?
These naughty Jack Russell's who've sinned.
Well they give us love and lots of fun,
and our blues have all Gone with the Wind.

Marie Little

ADAM'S FRESH FIGS

My Adam, he dumped me.
The serpent enticed,
So he hopped off elsewhere,
For his once, twice or thrice.

Contented for years,
I'd sit soft on his knee,
Whilst he temptingly served me
Fresh figs, from his tree.

He would wine me, would dine me,
With lush fruits, he'd entreat.
(Such a ripe juicy couple,
In Eden Vale Street.)

Now, exposed to the world,
My bereft naked soul,
At the height of fruit season
Is out of control.

Then I'm ranting, I'm raging,
Am shouting and screaming.
Folk think it's that seedy
Old lover I'm seeking.

No, being dumped by my Adam,
Doesn't matter to me.
But, oh! the craving I have
For fresh figs from his tree.

Honor Crellin

DAD

From November we had known
what your fate would be,
Your dying wish was to return to Wales
to be with your family.

Although you were not born here
this is home you'd say,
And this is where you wish to be
until that fated day.

Your main concern was for Mum
that she'd be settled here,
Surrounded by her loved ones
to help her through her fear.

Time passed by so quickly
you were weaker with each day,
They said you wouldn't make the journey
that you'd die along the way.

But what they did not know
was how determined you could be,
All you asked for was the chance
and left it to us three.

The next few days were spent
saying goodbye to all the family,
You had put your house in order
and it was time to let life be.

But there's one thing I regret
and on this you can depend,
I will always be so sorry Dad
because I wasn't there at the end.

Annette Owen

FUN IN THE SUN

Miss told us all to write about our summer holidays
I didn't quite know what to say, I haven't been away.
I've scrubbed and cleaned and washed the floors,
The kitchen cupboards, the wardrobe doors,
We've painted and papered in every room,
All except one, which will be done very soon.
I've done hours of work on my Apple Mac,
But of course that's to help me when I get back!
The best thing that happened? My daughter can drive,
The worst thing that happened? My brother-in-law died.
So what did I like best about my time at home?
My class could tell you - peace and quiet, being alone!
No more 'I've finished this, what shall I do now?'
'I'm stuck with my maths, will you show me how?'
'Ellen's got a nose-bleed, what shall we do?
It's splashed on her hands and is dripping on her shoe!'
'I've lost my pencil!' 'But you had it yesterday.'
'Yes and I know I put it in my tray when we packed away.'
'Tommy and Timmy are fighting, we thought you ought to know.'
But it's always like that with them, they're either friend or foe!
'There are only eight rubbers in the little red box.'
'We'll carry out a body search, they might be down their socks!'
And so it goes on, day after day after day,
It's so lovely and quiet when we have time away!
But the six weeks are over now, finished and done,
And a new class is waiting, oh, what fun!

Christine Naylor

THE AFTERGLOW

'He was a gentle man,' she said,
And showed his photograph.
It was golden-brown with age,
Showing a young man with a trombone.

His face was gentle,
Vulnerable, yet hopeful.
'He's gone now,' she said,
'but he was wonderful.
I loved him always.'

'I'm eighty-four,' she said,
Glowing gently, smiling without pain.
'He went three years ago, at eighty-seven.'
She showed another photograph.

It glowed with modern colour,
Showing an old couple together.
His face was still gentle, but old -
And there was no trombone.

'I've kept it polished,
And keep it safe,' she said.
'It was his pleasure,
Now it's mine.'

She stirred the heart
But not with pity,
The soul was awed,
At love transcended.

Pauline Boncey

OUR GARDEN

The ivy growing on the wall
And shrubs that tend to get too tall
There's dead flowers need the chop
And others that always flop
Grass that never stops growing
Must get on with the mowing
But it's all worthwhile.

Fruit of our labours to gather
Jobs we love and do together
Plums and veg and flowers too
Up they come in every hue
The earth yielding of its best
Time now for tea and a rest
Yet it's still worthwhile.

The seasons come and seasons go
Bringing with them sun, rain and snow
Time to dig and plant the crop
Before the snowdrops come up
Then daffodils put on a show
And all nature begins to grow
It's spring and worthwhile.

Now he has gone I'm all alone
To tend the garden on my own
The flowers bloom once again
Whether it's sunshine or rain
And the weeds come thick and fast
Not like the happy days past
Is it all worthwhile?

Margaret Earles

LONDON TRAIN TO HOLYHEAD

He seemed to shrink into the suede seat,
A slight man, with a parchment skin-tone.
Strangely, our eyes didn't meet
As he answered his mobile phone.
A rigid reflection haunted the black pane
As he glanced towards the station sign.
Straining into darkness from the slowing train,
He didn't look like a man in his prime.
'I'm in Stafford,' he said to the person at the end of the line.
'The train's an hour late into Holyhead,
Don't worry I'm feeling fine.'
Doors slammed, a whistle blew
Passengers packed their luggage away,
Noise in the carriage grew and grew.

Plastic coffee cups steamed on a tray,
Some people slept, chatted or read.
Picking up speed made everything sway
As into the night we sped.

The carriage emptied at Colwyn Bay,
Until the two of us sat alone.
'I've visited my daughter's grave today,'
The man spoke softly as we neared home.
'My wife she worries, I have cancer.
Soon she will be left on her own.
So I don't really know how to answer
Her fears, when she rings on the mobile phone!
It was our little girl's birthday, our only child.
I gave her fresh flowers, kissed her stone,
Told her she's not alone; at last she smiled!'

Jean Houghland

ACCIDENT PRONE

A man named Ned
Had a very large head
And a love of bananas
On boarding a boat
He was attacked by a stoat
And fell into a shoal of piranhas

'Enough' said Ned
As he swam the Med
And looked for his next adventure
'I'll just hop ashore
And look for some more'
And then had an attack of dementia

A passer-by
Said 'Quick he's going to die
Maybe we should call a paramedic'
But before they could
Up Ned stood
And then he started to leg it

Before ere long
Things went wrong
As he fell into a pillar-box
He was posted to
A liner's crew
And ended up washing their socks

They ran aground
As they found
That they were in Mozambique
A native man
Threw a boomerang
And Ned caught a fit of pique

Ian Harris

HOLIDAY BLUES

We had a long journey
and got there late,
to find only one caravan
booked to hold eight.
There were six left in our party,
with no bed for the night,
so they ended up going
half a mile off the site.
Those in the cottage
who were being messed around,
disapproved at first,
but were able to sleep sound.
However, those in the caravan,
were kept wide awake,
from being cramped and disturbed,
on hearing every noise you could make.
Whether it was having a shower,
or hearing somebody snore,
it meant the following night
the caravan only slept four.
For most of our party
went to the cottage off site,
just so we could have
a good sleep that night.
But, despite the commotion,
we had a good stay,
and came back refreshed
from a good holiday!

Wendy Moore

A Child's Tale

She walked along a country lane,
The summer days were hazy,
Evacuated with her family,
As all the world went crazy.

Her grandad was a teacher,
Her father, though ill, the best,
And with her family around her
She lived her life with zest.

She climbed stiles, ran through meadows,
Enjoyed days of snow and sun.
Then one sad night her daddy died,
Fighting against the Hun.

Her family cried, but the child grew,
To London they moved back,
11 plus, A' Levels, acting too,
She seemed to have the knack.

A shorthand course, and typing
Of which she was the best,
Awards galore she gathered up,
Ready to leave the nest.

The last job the child found,
At times when work was plenty,
Was with the 'Express', she loved the sound,
And by then she was twenty.

She met the man she was to wed
And is still with him today,
Grandparents, mother, now all dead,
But three children born, along the way.

And now five grandchildren live to see the wonder,
Because, years ago, Britain refused to go under.

Jill Silverman

THE INTERVIEW
(By a struggling artist)

The interview was set for twelve o'clock,
I told the receptionist in her middle-class frock,
She looked at me with her curly lip,
Then from her coffee she took a sip,
Minutes moved, a voice came over the air,
Miss McCarthy are you there?
Go to the showroom if you please,
Where you'll be met by our Miss Freeze.
In she came, looking like ice,
Full of apologies and too, too nice.
'Let me see what you've got,'
Hummed and ahhed about my lot,
'Not our house style not quite cute,
Here at Royle it would not suit.'
We only buy art that's going cheap,
'My dear, your portfolio is far too deep.
Why don't you try up the street.'

C C McCarthy